GUIDE TO THE
Gardens
OF South
Carolina

Other books by this author:

Guide to the Gardens of Florida

Guide to the Gardens of Georgia

GUIDE TO THE
Gardens
OF South
Carolina

LILLY PINKAS

PHOTOGRAPHS BY JOSEPH PINKAS

Line illustrations by Frank Lohan

PINEAPPLE PRESS, INC.
SARASOTA, FLORIDA

Acknowledgements

I would like to express express my sincere thanks to Dr. Brinsley Burbidge, Executive Director of Denver Botanic Gardens, for his respected advice and for his time in reviewing the manuscript. Special thanks to Mrs. Herbert A. Wood of Cayce, South Carolina, for her advice about historical facts concerning Memorial Garden. Many thanks to Mr. Ernest O. Shealy of Newberry, South Carolina, for his help in obtaining background information about Wells Japanese Garden. And the biggest thanks go to Lenka Wagner for editing the first drafts of the manuscript, a truly Herculean task, to say the least.

Pineapple Press, Inc.
P.O. Box 3889
Sarasota, Florida 34230

www.pineapplepress.com

Library of Congress Cataloging-in-Publication Data

Pinkas, Lilly.
      Guide to the gardens of South Carolina / Lilly Pinkas ; photographs by Joseph Pinkas.—1st ed.
         p.   cm.
      ISBN 1-56164-251-7 (pbk. : alk. paper)
       1. Gardens—South Carolina—Guidebooks. 2. South Carolina—Guidebooks. I. Title.

SB466.U65 S586 2002
712'.09757—dc21

                                        2001052089

First Edition
10 9 8 7 6 5 4 3 2 1

Design by Sandra Wright Designs
Printed in the United States of America

Table of Contents

continued

Foreword

It gets better and better. Lilly and Joe Pinkas have set themselves the daunting but, for those of us who love gardens, enviable task of systematically visiting every garden in the country and giving us their unbiased view on what they see. They have already given us outstanding guides to the gardens of Florida and Georgia and now they add South Carolina, a key state in the development of gardening as an art in the Americas. This book is another winner.

Their view is unapologetically that of experienced gardeners and therefore provides a very different perspective from most garden guides. But they add all the important information on history and setting that puts each garden in context. Lilly writes brilliantly and evocatively and it is easy to feel her enthusiasm for each of the gardens. It is easy to get on her wavelength and decide which of the gardens are a must for you. Even though I have visited only a few of the gardens, I know what the others are like just from the pleasurable experience of reading the text in draft. Her rare skill is complemented by Joe, who helps you confirm your choice with photographs that capture the essence of the gardens. Most important is that he sees the garden through a gardener's eyes and therefore extracts the perspective or view that the creator of the garden intended. As a team they are unbeatable.

Well researched, details are also here, especially how to get to the gardens. These directions actually work as the authors have driven to every garden, gotten lost, and figured out the best way of helping the rest of us get there.

Gardening has a great literary past and many gardeners write evocatively and passionately—usually about their own gardens. Something as humble as a visitors guide rarely gets the literary treatment, but here is the exception. Even if you never visit South Carolina you are in for a most enjoyable read—but I challenge you not to plan a visit after reading this. The state's gardens have already been honored in many excellent books. This guide gives equal attention to those, as well as many of the modest but equally rewarding places to visit. I love this book.

Dr. Brinsley Burbidge, Executive Director, Denver Botanic Gardens

Introduction

The thirty gardens described in this book are certainly a varied group. They range in size from a city garden on an eighth of an acre to a garden of several hundred acres. They include the garden that 260 years ago became the first formally landscaped garden in America, as well as a garden planted just a few years ago. Their origins are as varied as their present resources or their future goals. But whether their main purpose is to display, educate, research, or conserve, in their own special way they are oases of quiet peace and places of beauty and harmony in our increasingly complex, noisy, and hurried world.

We are confident that our list of gardens is comprehensive. We crisscrossed South Carolina many times in search of gardens and firmly believe we did not miss a single one. But if you find one that we missed, please write to us in care of the publisher so we can include it in the next edition. The thirty-two additional places mentioned are not gardens as such, but we feel they may be of interest to garden, plant, and nature lovers.

We gave a great deal of thought to the planning of our trips. Yes, we wanted to catch all the flowering peaks, but we also wanted to make some sense of our travels. Should we proceed from east to west or from north to south? It seemed obvious to start in Charleston, because this is where (in 1670) the first English colonists arrived to establish the first permanent English settlement in South Carolina. And it was here where, soon after their arrival, they established their experimental crop garden to see which crops would do well in this area. Later on, colonists ventured further inland so it seemed only logical for us to do the same.

We feel that including the proper travel directions certainly makes the trips easier and more enjoyable. A complete address and a phone number are given for each garden so you can inquire before you go concerning the best times to visit, flowering peaks, and any changes in the garden's hours.

We certainly hope that when you visit these gardens, you will have as much fun and see as much beauty as we did.

Coastal Region

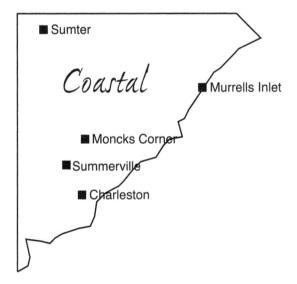

Sumter

Coastal

Murrells Inlet

Moncks Corner

Summerville

Charleston

This 738-acre plantation dates back to 1681, when Major Boone received 17,000 acres as a land grant. See the famous, half-mile, 250-year-old "Avenue of Oaks" on this, America's most-photographed plantation.

Address: P.O. Box 1554, Mount Pleasant, SC 29464

Directions: Take I-26 to its end. Continue on US 17 toward Mount Pleasant. After about 7 miles, the entrance to the plantation will be on your left.

Hours: April 1 to Labor Day: 8:30 a.m. to 6:30 p.m. Monday to Saturday; 1:00 p.m. to 5:00 p.m. Sunday. Rest of the year: 9:00 a.m. to 5:00 p.m. Monday to Saturday; 1:00 p.m. to 5:00 p.m. Sunday.

Closed: Thanksgiving and Christmas

Admission fee: yes

Wheelchair access: no

Facilities: restaurant, gift shop

Area: 738 acres

Phone: (843) 884-4371

Just about seven miles north of Charleston, on U.S. Highway 17 in Christ Church Parish, Boone Hall Plantation is rich in the history of South Carolina's low country.

The estate received its name from Maj. John Boone, a member of the first group of English settlers (known as "the First Fleet") who arrived in South Carolina in the late 1600s. In 1681, Major Boone received 17,000 acres as a land grant from the Lords Proprietors during the reign of King Charles II. The Boones were one of South Carolina's most influential families. Having strong ties to their native land, they later developed a deep loyalty to their new country. The daughter of Maj. John Boone, Sarah Boone, became the wife of Andrew Rutledge and the grandmother of Edward Rutledge, a signer of the Declaration of Independence, and John Rutledge, the first Governor of South Carolina.

Boone Hall Plantation was a cotton plantation in the eighteenth and nineteenth centuries, when cotton was king. The cotton produced on the plantation was taken to the gin house, where the cotton gin separated the fiber from the seed. The cotton fiber was then pressed into bales, loaded onto barges at the boat landing on the Wampacheone Creek, and then floated with the tide into Charleston Harbor to be exported all over the world. In 1817, the Boones sold the property to John and Henry Horlbeck, sons of Charleston's master builder, John Horlbeck. They established a large brick and tile works, and through the years Boone Hall Plantation was well known for its handmade bricks and tiles. Bricks made at the plantation were used in the construction of various buildings on the plantation, such as the gin house, the slave quarters, and the circular smoke house. Even the garden walks and walls are constructed of the same bricks, as are many of the historic houses in Charleston.

As the glory of cotton diminished, Boone Hall Plantation continued to diversify into other agricultural ventures. For example, it had one of the earliest commercial groves of pecans. Some of the trees planted by the Horlbecks still produce pecans today. At the present time, the pecan groves encompass more than 140 acres. Today, after three centuries, the Boone Hall Plantation remains privately owned, is thriving, and is still commercially productive.

As you approach the mansion, you pass under a canopy of massive, moss-draped oaks. And when you look down the one-half-mile oak avenue, you get a first glimpse of the majestic, brick plantation house, with its two-story, white-columned portico. This view through the oak allée is unforgettable. You are looking at America's most-photographed plantation, and you are also about to take a peek into a bygone era. Capt. Thomas Boone, a son of Maj. John Boone, planted the live oaks (*Quercus virginiana*) in 1743. He arranged the oaks in two, evenly spaced rows, and he made the allée so wide that it would take two hundred years for the branches to meet overhead.

Boone Hall's original plantation house was built in the mid-1700s. In 1935, the house was replaced by the present mansion. During the restoration, the lines of the original house were respected and enough of the original, handmade plantation bricks were found on the property for the restoration to be completed.

Formal gardens were planted in front of and along the flanks of the mansion. Each spring, the explosion of color is breathtaking. Hundreds of varieties of **azaleas** and **camellias** thrive here, and **Southern magnolias** blossom well into the early summer. The English-style garden, with **boxwood hedges** and brick walkways, is arranged in herringbone patterns to help define the traditional symmetry of the plantings. In the spring, thousands of **tulips** and other bulbs blend with the azalea and camellia plantings. Seasonal plantings of flowering plants enhance the formal gardens and provide color year round. When you visit, you will experience both beauty and history.

Calhoun Mansion

Formal gardens with water fountains and statuary surround this imposing Charleston mansion.

Address: 16 Meeting Street, Charleston, SC 29401
Directions: From I-95 take exit 86 and go east on I-26 until its end in the city of Charleston. Continue south on Meeting Street and the house will be on your left.
Hours: 10:00 a.m. to 4:00 p.m. Wednesday to Sunday
Closed: Thanksgiving and December 24–25
Admission fee: garden, no; house, yes
Wheelchair access: garden, yes; house, no
Facilities: none
Area: ¼ acre
Phone: (843) 722-8205

I n South Charleston, very close to The Battery, the Calhoun Mansion is widely acclaimed as one of the great houses of the Eastern seaboard. Wealthy, Southern merchant George Walton Williams, who spared no expense in design and construction, built this truly magnificent Victorian, 24,000-square-foot mansion in 1876. Williams' son-in-law, Patrick Calhoun, later acquired the property. Due to financial setbacks and reverses, he started to sell off some furnishings and eventually sold the mansion. There were nine subsequent owners of the property and it was used as a hotel, rooming house, and a private residence. But passing years were not kind to the mansion. By 1976, neglected and in disrepair, the mansion was boarded up and essentially devoid

of furnishings. A prominent local attorney, Gedney M. Howe III, acquired the property that year and set to restoring it to its former beauty and splendor. And he certainly succeeded, sparing no expense and giving extraordinary attention to every minute detail during the painstaking restoration process. The mansion is now open to the public as a house museum.

Surrounding the mansion on three sides, formal gardens complement the imposing structure. Brick pathways bordered by hedges of **boxwood** and **yew** will lead you past water fountains, cycads, and stately palmettos, with statuary artfully incorporated into the design. **Dogwoods, azaleas**, and **crape myrtles** provide color. During our visit we found a spectacular profusion of the yellow blossoms of **Lady Banksia rose** (*Rosa banksiae*) climbing the brick wall. The gardens are very pleasing yet dignified and are not to be missed.

Worth Seeing: Take a guided tour of the Calhoun Mansion. Enter through the massive walnut doors of this 24,000-square-foot mansion and you are in another world: an elegant ballroom; a music room with a 45-foot, covered glass skylight; a stairwell reaching to a 75-foot, domed ceiling; elaborate chandeliers. See one of the largest, eclectic collections of Victorian furnishings, museum-quality antiques, sculptures, fine art, Aubusson needlepoint tapestries, and much more.

Charles Towne Landing

Eighty acres of English Park Gardens await you on the site of the first permanent English settlement in South Carolina.

Address: 1500 Old Town Road, Charleston, SC 29407
Directions: From I-26 take exit 216A and go south on SC 7. After about 2 miles, bear left to connect with SC 171. From this point it is about 0.5 miles and the entrance will be on your left.
Hours: 9:00 a.m. to 6:00 p.m. daily from June to August; 9:00 a.m. to 5:00 p.m. daily from September to May
Admission fee: yes
Wheelchair access: yes
Facilities: restaurant, gift shop, and picnic areas
Available: tram tours, educational programs, and special events
Area: 664 acres
Phone: (843) 852-4200

Just a stone's throw northwest of Charleston, Charles Towne Landing is the site of the first permanent English settlement in South Carolina. Significant events in England preceded the arrival of settlers, the establishment of a colony, and the birth of Charleston. At the restoration of Charles II to the British throne in 1660, the eight Lords Proprietors had been rewarded for their loyalty and support of the king during the difficult times of the civil wars. Their reward was a vast tract of land on the little-known American Continent. After a long voyage (marred by storm, shipwreck, and death), the first English colonists arrived in 1670. And on this site in 1970 (in commemoration of South Carolina's tercentennial), Charles Towne Landing State Park was opened to the public. Today, displays at this state park interpret the first years of the colony's existence.

There are hundreds of acres of natural areas to explore. Start your visit in the theatre by watching a thirty-minute video entitled *Carolina*, which portrays life in the early South Carolina low country. Then you are ready either to take a thirty-minute, narrated Tram Tour that will give you an overview of the park, or start your own self-guided tour using the map you receive upon entering the park.

You can even explore on a bicycle, as there are miles of bicycle paths and bicycles are readily available for rental. And do not miss the nature trail that will allow you to see the natural progression of a forest.

We found our stroll through the eighty-acre gardens truly enjoyable—landscaped as English Park Gardens with lakes, tall **pines**, and stately, moss-draped **live oaks**. Some of these trees are said to be seven hundred to eight hundred years old. We enjoyed beautiful specimens of **crape myrtle, camellias,** and **loquats**. There is a profusion of blossoming **azaleas** and beautiful **dogwoods** in spring. And all of this in a peaceful, parklike setting. When you walk here, it feels like time is standing still.

The **1670 Experimental Crop Garden** is not to be missed. Here, early settlers experimented to find out what crops would grow well, for their own use or for export. Depending on the season, you can see rice, cotton, sugar cane, indigo, and many other crops. A step back into history, Charles Towne Landing is listed on the National Register of Historic Places.

Worth Seeing: The **Settlers' Life Area** is a reconstruction of a seventeenth-century village. Here you can get a feel for life in the seventeenth century. You can see a residence, woodworker's shop, smithy, and print shop. The grounds of this replica settlement are preserved for future archeological exploration.

The sailing vessel *Adventure* is a fifty-three-foot reproduction of a seventeenth-century, wooden trading ship. Explore the vessel above and below deck and try to visualize how it must have felt to sail across the ocean in this type of ship.

The **Animal Forest**, a twenty-acre, natural habitat zoo, features animals indigenous to South Carolina—the same animals that seventeenth-century settlers might have encountered. See bobcat, puma, wolves, bear, elk, deer, bison, red fox, alligator, and more.

The **Fortified Area** is the area of the original 1670 settlement, enclosed by earthen fortifications and palisade walls.

Drayton Hall

Drayton Hall is the only pre-Revolutionary–era plantation house on the Ashley River that survived the Civil War intact. It is located on 650 acres. Enjoy the stately live oaks, many of them three hundred years old. Encounter beauty as well as history.

Address: 3380 Ashley River Road, Charleston, SC 29414

Directions: From I-26 take exit 216A and go south on SC 7, which will become Sam Rittenberg Boulevard. Make a right turn onto Ashley River Road (SC 61) and continue north. After about 8 miles the entrance to the plantation will be on your right.

Hours: 10:00 a.m. to 4:00 p.m. daily from March to October; 10:00 a.m. to 3:00 p.m. from November to February

Closed: Thanksgiving, Christmas, New Year's Day, and at noon on both Christmas Eve and New Year's Eve

Admission fee: yes

Wheelchair access: partial

Facilities: gift shop

Available: educational programs, special events, lectures, and group tours by prior appointment

Area: 650 acres

Phone: (843) 769-2600 or (888) 349-0588

Located on the Ashley River near Charleston, Drayton Hall has more than its share of stories to tell. Once it was a plantation; now it is the site of the only pre-Revolutionary–era plantation house on the Ashley River that survived both the Revolutionary and Civil Wars intact. Since its completion in 1742, Drayton Hall represents the oldest surviving example of Georgian Palladian architecture in the southern United States.

John Drayton, born on the nearby Magnolia Plantation in 1713, knew he would not inherit his birthplace, so he purchased this adjoining tract of land in 1738. He immediately set about building a magnificent plantation house, which took four full years to complete. Years later, distinguished by the public offices he held, John Drayton became a Royal Judge and, at the time of his death, was considered to be one of the wealthiest men in the colony. He owned several rice-producing plantations and more than five hundred slaves. Drayton

Hall was his country seat, not a producing plantation. From here, he managed his other plantations and estates and enjoyed easy access to Charleston. His society friends visited him in his magnificent house, which was certainly built to impress. For the next 230 years, six generations of John Drayton's descendents continued to own Drayton Hall, many of them gaining national prominence. William Henry Drayton, John Drayton's eldest son, published a pamphlet signed "Freeman" shortly before the meeting of the first Continental Congress in 1774. It outlined a course of action for the Continental Congress and included a bill of rights. He also served in the 1778 Congress. After his death, Drayton Hall passed to his younger brother, Charles (1743–1820), a physician. Many descendents of the Drayton family were members of the medical profession.

Horticulture was the Drayton family's passion, and the greenhouse built in 1747 was the nucleus of Drayton's horticultural experiments. Many new plants and exotics were grown here and in surrounding gardens, to be tested for their introduction to the New World. Charles Drayton, who considered horticulture one of his diverse hobbies, kept a diary from 1779 until his death. In 1791, he planted varieties of olive trees and upland rice sent to him from France by Thomas Jefferson. In 1794 he met with renowned French botanist André Michaux, who was responsible for the introduction of many exotic plants to this country. From him he received plant specimens and advice.

The original landscape design, based on a precise geometric plan arranged along the central axis, was prevalent in eighteenth-century European gardens. In the Drayton Hall garden, the axis goes through the center of the house, down the oak avenue in front of the house, and through the garden lane to the Ashley River on the other side.

Throughout the ensuing years, the landscape and gardens underwent quite a few changes. During the Civil War years, tending the gardens was not of utmost importance. And it is said that the house itself escaped almost certain destruction by being posted with yellow flags signaling a

smallpox hospital, dissuading Union soldiers from coming close enough to torch it. At the end of the nineteenth century, the garden landscape was more parklike, with plantings of young trees and swept paths. At this same time the reflection pond was constructed. The excavated dirt was used to create the garden mound in front of the house. At the turn of the twentieth century, plantings of azaleas and camellias were added. The National Trust acquired the property from the Drayton family for historic preservation in 1974.

Little of the original landscape exists today, and there are no formal gardens left. At the present time, the primary attractions of this plantation-style garden are stately **live oaks**, some of them three hundred years old, and **azaleas** and **camellias** adding color in the spring and fall. The house, now standing alone, seems almost austere. You just have to imagine its flankers, an assortment of outbuildings and even a solar-heated orangérie to house citrus trees.

You can explore the grounds of Drayton Hall by taking one of two self-guided walks: either the thirty-minute River Walk or the forty-five-minute Marsh Walk. In this parklike setting, you will encounter serenity and beauty.

Worth Seeing: On your tour of Drayton Hall, you will see a marvelous example of Colonial architecture that stands in nearly original condition. It is preserved but not restored. Seven generations of Draytons never disturbed the house by adding plumbing, electricity, or heating. The decision was made to leave the house unfurnished to better demonstrate its architectural craftsmanship. The house is the oldest surviving example of Georgian Palladian architecture in the southern United States. Its two-story portico is believed to be the first of its type in America. Palladian architecture flourished in Georgian England and was based on classical use of order, symmetry, regularity, and uniformity, where principal rooms were symmetrically arranged around a spacious great hall. The skill of unnamed craftsmen of long ago is obvious and amazing: from hand-carved plaster ceilings, to elaborately carved mahogany spindles of stairway banisters, to ornamentation featuring egg-and-dart and bead-and-reel moldings. And the list could go on and on. Guided tours of the house are conducted every hour. The Connoisseur Tour is offered by appointment only and offers more detailed information about architecture, decorative arts, and the social history of the house.

Heyward-Washington House

Built by Daniel Heyward, this is probably the best-known house in Charleston. The small garden gracing the grounds is not to be missed.

Address: 87 Church Street, Charleston, SC 29401
Directions: From I-95 take exit 86 and go east on I-26 until its end in the city of Charleston. Continue south on Meeting Street, then make a left turn onto Broad Street. Go east, make a right turn onto Church Street, and the house will be on your right.
Hours: 10:00 a.m. to 5:00 p.m. Monday to Saturday; 1:00 p.m. to 5:00 p.m. Sunday
Closed: Easter, Thanksgiving, Christmas Day, and New Year's Day
Admission fee: yes
Wheelchair access: house, no; garden, yes
Facilities: none
Area: ¼ acre
Phone: (843) 722-0354 or (843) 722-2996

The Heyward-Washington House is probably one of the best known in this city, and the gardens located behind it are very much loved and admired. The house was built in 1772 by Daniel Heyward, whose son, Thomas Heyward Jr., was a delegate to the Continental Congress and also a signer of the Declaration of Independence. While visiting Charleston in May of 1791, President George Washington stayed in the house for about ten days and ever since, the house has been referred to as the Heyward-Washington House. In 1794, the property was purchased by Judge John F. Grimke, who lived there with his family until 1803; the Grimke sisters of abolitionist fame were born there. The house was used as a boarding house throughout most of the nineteenth century. In 1929 it was acquired by the Charleston Museum and at that time there remained no garden to speak of.

In 1931, Mrs. Emma B. Richardson, Assistant Director of the Charleston Museum, was given the task of recreating a late eighteenth-century garden. Since George Washington had resided in the house, it was decided to use only plants that were in cultivation prior to 1791. The collection of heirloom plants certainly adds to the historic character of this garden. Some of the plants received for use in the garden were **crape myrtle** (*Lagerstroemia indica*), **jessamine** (*Gelsemium sempervirens*), **lantana** (*Lantana camara*), **gardenia** (*Gardenia jasminoides*), **Cherokee rose** (*Rosa laevigata*), and **woodbine** (*Lonicera sempervirens*), just to mention a few. After consulting many old garden plans, Mrs. Richardson developed an attractive, eighteenth-century, geometric design, using brick-bordered beds with concentric paths. Further refinements in the design and plantings of the garden were implemented in 1965 with the advice of landscape architect Loutrel Briggs and the efforts of the Garden Club of Charleston.

In 1989, Charleston was ravaged by the fury of Hurricane Hugo. The damage was quite extensive and the gardens of the Heyward-Washington House did not escape unscathed, with a portion of the garden being destroyed by the storm. Once again, the Garden Club of Charleston replanted the garden, this time as an eighteenth-century knot garden. The rectangular, brick-walled garden with a circular bed at the center is surrounded by additional geometrically shaped beds. An extensive herb garden contains **foxglove** (*Digitalis purpurea*), **rue** (*Galega officinalis*), **valerian** (*Valeriana officinalis*), and **calendula** (*Callendula officinalis*), as well as many **old-fashioned roses**. If you visit in the spring, you will immediately notice the heavy fragrance of **gardenias** (*Gardenia jasminoides*) and the **banana shrub** (*Michelia figo*) that permeates the garden. **Boxwood** hedges and red brick paths will lead you and invite you to explore further. Many species of flowering shrubs and **native ferns** are planted alongside the back wall. This garden is certainly one to be enjoyed.

Worth Seeing: Tour the Heyward-Washington House, the only eighteenth-century house museum in the city of Charleston with a kitchen building open to the public. The house contains a valuable collection of eighteenth-century, Charleston-made furniture, which includes the priceless Holmes bookcase, considered to be the finest example of American-made furniture in existence. And do not forget to see the kitchen of the Heyward-Washington House. It was probably constructed around 1740. Keep in mind that cooking at that time was done over an open hearth and that fire was a constant hazard. That is why kitchens were usually located away from the main house. This also kept the house cool and free from cooking odors.

Joseph Manigault House

The ornamental Gate Temple enhances the garden of this neoclassical house, which is a National Historic Landmark.

Address: 350 Meeting Street, Charleston, SC 29403
Directions: From I-95 take exit 86 and go east on I-26 until its end
   in the city of Charleston. Continue south on Meeting Street and
   the house will be on your left.
Hours: 10:00 a.m. to 5:00 p.m. Monday to Saturday; 1:00 p.m. to
   5:00 p.m. Sunday
Closed: Easter Sunday, Thanksgiving, Christmas Day, and New
   Year's Day
Admission fee: grounds, no; house, yes
Wheelchair access: garden, yes; house, no
Facilities: none
Area: ¼ acre
Phone: (843) 723-2926

The mid-sixteenth century was quite tumultuous in France, and the Huguenots (French Protestants) were severely persecuted under Kings Francis I and Henry II. They survived the attempt to exterminate them (the Massacre of St. Bartholomew in 1572) as well as the religious wars of the next thirty years. In 1598, Henry IV granted them toleration under the Edict of Nantes. But Louis XIV revoked this edict in 1685, attempting to force their conversion. This resulted in the emigration of 400,000 Huguenots.

Pierre Manigault was one of the Huguenots fleeing religious persecution. Arriving in Charleston around 1695, he joined other Huguenots farming around the Santee River. Not satisfied with farming, he returned to Charleston and established various business interests, including two brandy distilleries. His son Gabriel, who inherited and further enlarged his father's mercantile interests, became one of the region's richest merchants, involved in a wide-ranging import and export enterprise. By the mid-1730s, the production and export of rice were extremely profitable, greatly enhancing the wealth of the colony. Gabriel's son, Peter Manigault (1731–1773), after the customary education in Europe, embarked on a distinguished political career in the Commons House of Assembly. Peter's sons, Gabriel and Joseph (also educated in Europe), returned to tend to their plantations and other varied business interests, which were considerable. It is said they inherited about 40,000 acres and five hundred slaves. Gabriel Manigault (a talented, self-taught architect) set about designing a house for his brother. He is also credited with designing other Charleston structures.

In the early 1800s, Charleston was a vibrant city of 20,000. Commerce was thriving and ships laden with cargoes of rice and cotton were leaving the port constantly. It was also the time for wealthy planters and merchants to build their elegant houses in the city. The Joseph Manigault House was constructed between 1803 and 1807 and represents a premier example of neoclassical architecture. The influence of the Scottish architect Robert Adam (who, in the late eighteenth century, introduced neoclassical elements to British architecture) is apparent throughout the house. It is believed that during his studies in England, Gabriel Manigault became interested in Adam's work. The ornamental Gate Temple enhancing the garden was completed in 1803 and is reminiscent of classical temples popular in English and French gardens of that time. Its bell-shaped, circular roof and its pedimental portico make this structure unique in Charleston.

The Manigault family occupied the house until 1852 when it was sold. One of Charleston's earliest preservation groups, the Society for the Preservation of Old Dwellings, recognized the historical and architectural significance of the Joseph Manigault House and focused on saving it. With donated funds, the Charleston Museum was able to purchase the house in 1933 and opened it to the public in 1949. It was designated a National Historic Landmark in 1974.

Joseph Manigault's wife, Charlotte, designed the original garden. The garden as we see it today basks in abundant sunshine as there is not much of a shade-providing canopy. Brick-

lined gravel pathways, **boxwood** hedges, and an expanse of lawn (all laid out in symmetry along the main axis) run from the Gate Temple to the main entry of the house. **Azaleas** planted along the brick walls provide pleasing color in spring, as does the **dogwood**. Later on, **African lilies**, **hydrangeas**, and **oleanders** take their turn. This garden is a quiet oasis just a step away from the busy streets of the city.

Magnolia Plantation and Gardens ❀

Named after the long allée of magnolias that once stretched from the mansion to the Ashley River, Magnolia Plantation is the site of America's oldest garden. After more than three hundred years, it is still one of the most beautiful and magnificent of America's gardens. Just come and see for yourself.

Address: Ashley River Road, Charleston, SC 29414

Directions: From I-26 take exit 216A and go south on SC 7, which will become Sam Rittenberg Boulevard. Make a right turn onto Ashley River Road (SC 61) and continue north. After about 9.5 miles the entrance to the plantation will be on your right.

Hours: 8:00 a.m. to 5:00 p.m. daily

Admission fee: yes

Wheelchair access: yes

Facilities: gift shop, snack shop, gallery of American nature and wildlife artists

Available: memberships, guided bird walks

Area: 500 acres

Phone: (843) 571-1266

Not far from Charleston, bounded by the Ashley River, the Magnolia Plantation is the site of the first plantation house of significance in this region as well as the site of America's oldest garden. It is named for the long allée of magnolias that once stretched from the mansion to the Ashley River. Over three centuries ago, Magnolia Plantation became the first home to the American branch of the Drayton family. This prominent family, whose roots go all the way back to the Norman Conquest of England, played an important role in the making of America. In the mid-1600s, Thomas Drayton, together with his son, Thomas Jr., left England for a new life in Barbados. After several years there, they decided to settle in the new colony of Carolina. The original plantation house (which was built in 1670 for Thomas Drayton Jr. and his wife) burned accidentally. About half a century later, a second house met the same fate when it was burned to the ground by General Sherman's troops in 1865. The house standing at Magnolia Plantation today is a pre-

Revolutionary summer house that was owned by Rev. John Grimke Drayton of Summerville, fourteen miles up the Ashley River. After the plantation house was burned, he disassembled his summer house, loaded it on barges, floated it to Magnolia, and in 1873 had it reassembled on the site of the burned-out ruins of the original house.

Gardens were part of the original plan for the plantation and initially covered only about ten acres. Today, not much remains of the original formal gardens except a small section dating from the 1680s, known as Flowerdale. As the gardens grew, each generation of owners left its imprint on the landscape. The gardens, as they appear today, were redesigned by Rev. John Grimke Drayton. He decided to change the original, French-influenced design (with its formality and manicured symmetry) and convert it to a more pastoral, softer, informal, English landscape design. Along with the extensive plantings of exotic trees and shrubs, lakes and ponds were created and romantic winding paths and wooden bridges were constructed.

The first specimens of Southern Indian Azalea (*Azalea indica*) were planted here about 1843. Southern Indian Azaleas are native to Japan and China. Originally introduced to Europe, hybrids were developed in England and eventually found their way to America. In the North they were grown in greenhouses and later introduced as outdoor plants in the South. Rev. Drayton also imported many varieties of camellias (*Camellia japonica*). It is believed that in the 1860s there were more than 120 varieties of camellias growing in the gardens.

The Reverend's plans for developing the gardens into an earthly paradise were undoubtedly cut short by the Civil War. The war devastated most of the plantations in the Charleston area, but the gardens at Magnolia Plantation miraculously survived. Although the plantation house was burned to the ground, the gardens were essen-

tially untouched. After the Civil War, Rev. Drayton was nearly desti-
tute. Out of financial necessity he opened Magnolia Gardens to the
public in 1870, thus making them not only America's oldest garden
but also America's oldest, man-made tourist attraction. Magnolia
Plantation has been in continuous ownership by the Drayton family
for nine generations since 1670. Today the plantation is directed by
its owner with no compensation. The owner pays full taxes and
accepts no contributions, and all receipts are reinvested in the property to enhance its beauty for future generations.

Start your visit at the Orientation Theater with a twelve-minute,
color video that highlights the history of the plantation. Your admission ticket is also your map, so you are ready to start your self-
guided tour by following the numbered signs along the pathways. As
with any Southern garden, the Magnolia Gardens are at their best in
the spring. Under a canopy of moss-draped **live oaks** (*Quercus
virginiana*) the display of blooms is spectacular. **Azaleas** (*Azalea
indica*), **yellow jessamine** (*Gelsemium sempervirens*), **wisteria** (*Wisteria
sinensis*) and the **Cherokee rose** (*Rosa laevigata*) all show off their
beauty. Extensive introductions of other flowering plants over the
years have not only enhanced the gardens' beauty but also transformed them into a paradise, where arrays of color can be enjoyed
year round. Summer visitors are greeted with blossoms of **magnolias**
(*Magnolia grandiflora*), **gardenias** (*Gardenia jasminoides*),
bougainvillea (*Bougainvillea spectabilis*), and **tea olives** (*Osmanthus
fragrans*). Fall brings colors of **lantana** (*Lantana camara*), **yellow
cassia** (*Cassia splendida*), and **hibiscus** (*Hibiscus rosa-sinensis*). Winter
is an exciting time to visit as well. The profusion of
berries, hollies, cherries,
and **plums** certainly
adds additional
colors to the winter
landscape. And, of
course, in late
winter and early
spring, several
hundred vari-
eties of
camellias
show off their

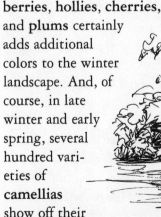

pink, white, and red blossoms. Today, Magnolia Plantation boasts one of the largest outdoor collections of camellias and azaleas in the United States, approaching 1,200 varieties.

There is so much to see here. The **Maze Garden**, with its almost quarter mile of pathways, was patterned after the maze designed by Henry VIII at his Hampton Court estate in the sixteenth century. Instead of the usual boxwood, the Magnolia's maze has been planted with five hundred camellias combined with holly. And what fun not only trying to find your way *in* to the center square, but also trying to find your way *out*.

Magnolia's **Herb Garden** follows the seventeenth-century design by planting herbs in small beds surrounding the formal, boxwood knot garden. In Colonial days, every plantation had its own herb garden for the kitchen as well as for medicinal use. Great care was taken to plant this garden as attractively as possible.

Another treat to enjoy is the 7,000-square-foot **Barbados Tropical Garden Greenhouse** planted with tropical plants indigenous to Barbados. Barbados was the Drayton family's ancestral home in the New World. The small **Topiary Garden** is waiting to be enjoyed as well. The **Biblical Garden**, planted exclusively with plants mentioned in the Bible, is divided into two sections: Old and New Testaments. In the New Testament section, plants and flowers are planted in twelve sections around the cross, representing the twelve disciples. In the Old Testament section, the Star of David is made up of twelve sections, commemorating the twelve tribes of Israel.

There is a 125-acre rice field, now a waterfowl refuge, complete with a wildlife observation tower. Multiple nature trails crisscross the plantation and offer many vantage points from which to observe the wildlife. The entire five hundred acres of the Magnolia Plantation have been managed as a wildlife refuge since 1975.

The **Audubon Swamp Garden** is one of the country's newest major gardens. It is comprised of sixty acres of blackwater swamp that were originally used as a freshwater reservoir for the plantation's rice fields. In the 1830s, the great ornithologist and bird artist, John J. Audubon, visited here to observe water birds as a guest of Rev. Dr. John Drayton, the plantation owner at that time.

It is not easy to describe the feelings one experiences when visiting here. Even on a beautiful, sunny day, this eerie landscape is outright mysterious, but at the same time, the colors of hundreds of species of flowering plants reassure you that this is a peaceful place. As you stroll along the walkways under the canopy of **water oaks** (*Quercus nigra*), **tupelos** or **black gums** (*Nyssa sylvatica*), and **sweet gums** (*Liquidambar styraciflua*), you can admire **bold cypress** (*Taxodium distichum*) reflecting their images in the still swamp with their knees sticking out of the water all around them. Wherever you look, there is something to see: **cattails** and **wildflowers** at the edge of the swamp, **ornamental grasses** by the walkways, **water lilies** and **bog plants** in the swamp itself. The series of walkways, bridges, boardwalks, and dikes will enable you to explore this wild and otherwise inaccessible acreage, and to observe and enjoy not just the native and exotic plants, but also the wildlife. More than 220 bird species are found here, as well as many water-loving animals and reptiles. You will discover that most of the low-country wildlife will be oblivious to your presence.

When you visit here, you'd better save at least half a day. There is so much to see and marvel at. Without question, Magnolia Plantation, which is listed on the National Register of Historic Places, is one of the most beautiful and magnificent of America's gardens. And looking at more than three hundred years of its past, we sense that the future will be bright and will bring even more beauty.

Worth Seeing: A tour of the Magnolia Plantation house highlights the history of the Drayton family and exhibits an outstanding collection of Early American furniture. See a restored, pre-Revolutionary rice barge, a "street" of antebellum cabins, a large Indian burial mound, and a petting zoo of plantation animals.

A forty-five-minute **Nature Train** ride will take you on a tour outside the historic garden, through the wildlife refuge bordering the Ashley River, and through the historic rice fields. There are five miles of nature trails crisscrossing the wildlife refuge.

Middleton Place

Middleton Place is nationally and internationally recognized for its historical significance and beauty. Overlooking the Ashley River, it is home to America's oldest, formal, landscaped gardens dating back to 1741. Come and visit this landscaping masterpiece.

Address: 4300 Ashley River Road, Charleston, SC 29414

Directions: From I-26 take exit 216A and go south on SC 7, which will become Sam Rittenberg Boulevard. Make a right turn onto Ashley River Road (SC 61) and continue north. After about 16 miles the entrance to the plantation will be on your right.

Hours: 9:00 a.m. to 5:00 p.m. daily

Closed: Thanksgiving and Christmas

Admission fee: yes

Wheelchair access: partial

Facilities: restaurant, museum shop, inn

Available: membership

Area: 110 acres

Phone: (843) 556-6020 or (800) 782-3608

Just a few miles northwest of Charleston, situated on the western banks of the Ashley River, lies Middleton Place, home of America's oldest, formal, landscaped garden. The land was originally settled in the late 1600s. Henry Middleton acquired the house (with some two hundred surrounding acres) in 1741 as part of his wife's dowry. Henry Middleton was, however, immensely wealthy in his own right. It is believed that he owned about twenty plantations and was Carolina's largest landowner, with holdings of at least 50,000 acres. The Middletons were not just wealthy landowners; they were also important citizens in the early days of this country. Middleton Place continued to serve as the family seat of four successive generations. Henry Middleton was president of the First Continental Congress. His son, Arthur, was president of the convention that overthrew the Lords Proprietors and was also a signer of the Declaration of Independence. Arthur's son, Henry, was governor of South Carolina and minister to Russia. Henry's son, Williams, signed the Ordinance of Secession, which aimed to destroy the Union less than one hundred years after the birth of the Union, which his great-grandfather and grandfather had helped to create.

The original house—a three-story, brick structure three hundred feet long—was built in 1705. A pair of flankers was added around 1755. The house was plundered during the Revolution and then burned by General Sherman's army at the end of the Civil War in 1865. As if this were not enough, the earthquake of 1886 toppled what was left of the ruins, except for the bachelor's quarters. The earthquake also severely damaged the plantation's intricate irrigation system and emptied both Butterfly Lakes. Overall, the gardens suffered less misfortune than the house.

Henry Middleton had begun to create the gardens in 1741. He envisioned a great and elegant garden—one of such size and beauty that none other in America at that time could match it. And he succeeded, creating gardens of such grandeur that no one else in America would attempt anything like it for the next several generations. His garden design reflects the influence of the landscaping style prevalent in the great gardens of early eighteenth-century Europe. He was undoubtedly inspired by André Le Notre, the famous seventeenth-century French landscape designer responsible for designing Louis XIV's gardens at Versailles, as well as many other great European gardens. But there are also elements of a freer, English garden design, so that both styles are represented here.

In the style of seventeenth-century France, each garden was based on a precise, geometric plan consisting of a central axis along which the other elements of design—such as terraces, reflecting pools, and paths—were arranged. The view along the primary axis would always stretch far into the distance, suggesting that the garden owner's power and control stretched that far as well. Geometry, symmetry, and logic were responsible for bringing formality into the French garden design, with trees set in straight lines and topiary topped or so greatly pruned that the final shape was more geometrical than natural. The hills were reshaped or removed altogether and replaced by flat parterres. Water was confined in precisely geometrical pools. In short, nature was controlled—forced to conform to design.

The English garden, which at first glance appears quite informal with its looseness of planting and abundance of flowers, is actually quite structured. Its formality is contained within an apparently natural landscape.

Henry Middleton laid out the gardens in a formal symmetry, with the main axis running from the entrance gate, through the central hall of the main house, descending to where the parterres and curving terraces would be built, between the Butterfly Lakes that would be dug, and extending into the Ashley River and marshes beyond. The formal garden, which lies northwest of the house, is based on an exact right triangle and is situated at a right angle to this axis. The design is perfectly adapted to the contours of the land. With the help of a professional gardener from England, the enormous landscaping project began. Two matching, artificial lakes (resembling a pair of butterfly wings) were dug out of the soft soil. The excavated soil was then used to form symmetrical, descending terraces. The Rice Mill Pond was created by damming the natural creek. All of this was part of an intricate and elaborate irrigation system that not only supplied water for the Butterfly Lakes but also irrigated the rice fields. It is said to have taken one hundred slaves almost ten years of continuous labor to create the artificial lakes, terraces, and walks and to finally complete the project.

Each generation of Middletons left their mark on the landscape. But whether they introduced new plantings or added color to the landscape, they essentially followed the original gardening plan. Henry Middleton II added further plantings to the gardens. He was a friend of the famous French botanist André Michaux, who introduced many new exotic plants to America. Michaux visited Middleton Place in 1786, and the four camellias (*Camellia japonica*) he brought with him were the first to be planted in an American garden. Williams Middleton further enhanced the gardens by planting multitudes of azaleas (*Azalea indica*).

The Civil War brought the golden era of Middleton Place to an abrupt end. For many years following the Civil War, the gardens were neglected and overgrown. But they survived. At the beginning of the twentieth century, work was started to restore the gardens to their former magnificence and beauty. In the 1930s, the hillside above Rice Mill Pond was planted with 35,000 azaleas of many varieties and colors. The restoration efforts were more than successful, and the beauty can again be seen everywhere. In 1941, Middleton Place won the prestigious and coveted Bulkey Medal bestowed by the Garden Club of America. It proclaimed Middleton Place "the most interesting and important Garden in America . . . in commemoration of 200 years of enduring beauty."

The restored gardens were designated a National Historic Landmark in 1971. The property is owned by The Middleton Place Foundation, which was established in 1974 in order to form and administer the policies of preservation and conservation. The gardens were opened to the public in 1975.

The entrance to the formal gardens is from the west. One immediately encounters the long and narrow, spring-fed **Reflection Pool**. Magnificent **Southern magnolias** (*Magnolia grandiflora*) and **live oaks** (*Quercus virginiana*) tower nearby and reflect their images in the water. **Camellia allées** run from the southern end of the Reflection Pool to the east, toward the Ashley River. The formal garden is divided by perpendicular and parallel paths and allées into several distinct, smaller gardens. When walking the garden paths, you just keep discovering additional gardens partitioned off by walls of greenery. You can explore the **Secret Gardens** or **Sundial Garden**. The **Octagonal Garden** is beautiful; the fragrant **sweet olives** (*Osmanthus fragrans*) were planted there in the 1850s. The **Rose Garden** holds specimens of **tea roses** and **China roses** first propagated here in the eighteenth and nineteenth centuries. The **crape myrtle** (*Lagerstroemia indica*) here are some of the largest in this country. (André Michaux introduced this beautiful, oriental flowering tree here.) Other examples of his introductions are the **mimosa tree** (*Albizia julibrissin*), **ginkgo tree** (*Ginkgo biloba*), and **candleberry tree** (*Sapium sebiferum*). The four **camellias** (*Camellia japonica*) Michaux brought in 1786 were planted at each corner of the parterre. One of them is still living and is called *Reine des Fleurs* (Queen of Flowers). The **Green Walks** along the south and north borders of the main parterre contain many interesting specimens of several varieties of **magnolias**. The **New Camellia Garden** contains many varieties of camellias, including **tea** *(Camellia sinensis),* planted mostly in the 1940s.

Throughout the property, the predominant tree is the **live oak** (Quercus virginiana), and some of the most magnificent specimens can be seen here. On the bluff overlooking the Ashley River stands the **Middleton Oak**. This live oak, believed to be 1,000 years old, stands eighty-five feet tall and has a limb spread of 145 feet and a circumference of over 37 feet. Besides oaks, a variety of other trees can be enjoyed: **American beech** *(Fagus grandifolia),* **hickory** *(Carya spp.),* **tulip poplar** *(Liriodendron tulipifera),* **eastern red cedar** *(Juniperis virginiana),* **Southern red cedar** *(Juniperis silicicola),* and **sweet gum** *(Liquidambar styraciflua),* just to mention a few. In the spring, the colors of flowering trees are spectacular. The pink blossoms of **redbud trees** *(Cercis canadensis)* and the white blossoms of **dogwood trees** *(Cornus florida)* are just amazing. And then there are **azaleas**. Thousands of azaleas grow on the hillside above the **Rice Mill Pond**. Still more azaleas can be enjoyed around the **Azalea Pool,** and native azaleas thrive in the woods beyond the **Bamboo Grove**. Around **Cypress Lake** one can quietly enjoy the plants indigenous to this area, such as **atamasco lily** *(Zephyranthes atamasco)* and **winter daphne** *(Daphne odora).*

The flowering peaks obviously vary with the seasons, but there is color in the gardens year round. The color, however, is just part of the picture. Middleton Place truly is a landscaping masterpiece, and a visit here is a special experience. While admiring the present beauty, we also get a sense of the past and a glimpse into an era that is no more.

Worth Seeing: A guided tour of the Middleton Place House Museum gives visitors additional insight into the lives of generations of Middletons. Open to the public since 1975, the house museum contains family furniture, English silver, most of the original china, paintings, books, letters, and documents. Most of the objects here date from the 1740s to 1880s. Keep in mind that the remaining building here is the restored south flanker. The main house and the north flanker were damaged beyond repair when Union troops torched them on February 22, 1865.

Plantation Stableyards. A visit here will underscore the fact that a plantation truly was a self-sufficient community. Almost everything needed on a plantation was produced right here. See the animals that were so vital to plantation life. See the blacksmith and carpentry shops. See how tools, pottery, soap, candles, and fabric were made by hand.

Nathaniel Russell House

Spacious, formal gardens surround this house, one of America's most important Federal period townhouses.

Address: 51 Meeting Street, Charleston, SC 29401
Directions: From I-95 take exit 86 and go east on I-26 until its end in the city of Charleston. Continue south on Meeting Street and the house will be on your left.
Hours: 10:00 a.m. to 4:30 p.m. Monday to Saturday; 2:00 p.m. to 4:30 p.m. Sunday
Closed: major holidays
Admission fee: garden, no; house, yes
Wheelchair access: garden, yes; house, no
Facilities: gift shop
Area: ¼ acre
Phone: (843) 724-8481

Born in Bristol, Rhode Island, Nathaniel Russell arrived in Charleston in 1765 at the age of twenty-seven as an agent for Providence merchants. Near the wharves he also ran a store of his own that steadily prospered. His marriage to Sarah Hopton, daughter of one of Charleston's wealthy merchants, enhanced his standing even further and he eventually became the richest Charleston merchant of the post-Revolutionary period. The construction of his splendid mansion on Meeting Street started in 1803 and was completed in the spring of 1808. This mansion is recognized as one of the most important, neoclassical dwellings of Federal-period architecture. No architect was ever credited with the design, however, and it is believed that Russell himself quite possibly did the architectural drawings. According to others, the mansion was designed by Charleston's gentleman architect, Gabriel Manigault.

Nathaniel Russell died in 1820, having enjoyed his spectacular mansion for only twelve years. The house stayed in the family until 1857 when it was purchased by Gov. R.F.W. Allston, who, as it was widely believed, was the richest planter in South Carolina. After the governor's death, the house was converted into a girls' school and sold again in 1870 to the Sisters of Charity of Our Lady of Mercy to

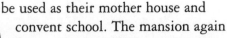

be used as their mother house and convent school. The mansion again became a private residence and continued as such until 1955. In that year, the Historic Charleston Foundation acquired the house, which (after extensive renovation) was opened as a house museum in 1956.

Brick walls and a wrought-iron fence surround the formal gardens of the Nathaniel Russell House. Through the iron gate you enter the smaller front garden east of the house. Follow the gravel and brick paths bordered by hedges of **boxwood** and **yew** under the shade of **Southern magnolias** and **live oaks** into the larger garden along the south side of the house. Blossoms of **azaleas** and **dogwoods** provide pleasing color early in spring, followed by colorful blooms of **lilies, hydrangeas**, and **roses. Gardenias** show off their blossoms and the intense fragrance permeates the air. As you enjoy the garden, you will discover small statues, iron benches, and plantings in urns in shady nooks.

Worth Seeing: Take a guided tour of the Nathaniel Russell House, which contains a valuable collection of eighteenth-century Charleston- and English-made furniture, as well as period furnishings. See the oval, rectangular, and square rooms (designed with exquisite moldings) on each of the three floors. The staircase here is probably the grandest of its type surviving in Charleston. The swirling, free-flying staircase that rises three stories seems to have no visible support. It was built using the cantilever principle: each step is supported by the step just below it and by each landing. The curving handrail is of fine, Honduras mahogany.

Philip Simmons Garden

Come and enjoy this small garden with an intriguing topiary, right in the heart of Charleston.

Address: 91 Anson Street, Charleston, SC 29401

Directions: From I-95 take exit 86 and go east on I-26 until its end in the city of Charleston. Continue south on Meeting Street, make a left turn onto George Street, go one block, make a left turn onto Anson Street, go one block, and make a left turn onto Menotti Street. The parking lot of St. John Reformed Episcopal Church and the garden entrance will be on your left.

Hours: sunrise to sunset daily

Admission fee: none

Wheelchair access: yes

Facilities: none

Area: ¼ acre

Phone: no phone

This small, young, and quite unusual garden is located in the heart of Charleston. The Philip Simmons Foundation spearheaded the development of the garden, which was opened in 1997. Over the span of more than six decades during the twentieth century, Philip Simmons (a master blacksmith who used his talent and his simple tools) built some of the most beautiful iron gates in Charleston. Loved in Charleston and also nationally acclaimed, Simmons was honored by the National Endowment for the Arts with its highest award for folk artists. One of his gates was purchased by the Smithsonian to be included in their collections. Philip Simmons created the heart and cross design of the garden entry gates, as well as the ornamental wall piece

depicting his vision of Charleston. The topiary was designed by topiary artist Pearl Fryar. This garden is also known as the Heart Garden because, in addition to the hearts in the gates, there are heart inlays in walkways and a heart design in the showpiece swan topiary. Adjacent to the brick structure of St. John Reformed Episcopal Church, this walled garden has its own identity. Enjoy the **topiary** creations and the plantings of **roses** along the walls as you stroll the brick-bordered pathways of this uncommon garden.

Cypress Gardens

Cypress Gardens comprises 175 acres of a blackwater wonderland of cypress and tupelo forest. Walk the paths or go by boat; admire water lilies, azaleas, camellias, dogwoods, and daffodils.

Address: 3030 Cypress Gardens Road, Moncks Corner, SC 29461
Directions: From I-26 take exit 208 and go north on US 52 past
  Goose Creek. Follow the signs and make a right turn onto
  Cypress Gardens Road. The gardens will be on your right.
Hours: 9:00 a.m. to 5:00 p.m. daily
Closed: Thanksgiving, Christmas, and month of January
Admission fee: yes
Wheelchair access: yes
Facilities: gift shop, visitors center
Available: educational programs, season passes, special group rates
Area: 175 acres
Phone: (843) 553-0515

Tucked away in the quiet Carolina countryside, the Cypress Gardens (unique swamp gardens) are rich in natural beauty. The site on which the gardens are located was originally part of the 3,000-acre Dean Hall Plantation, one of the largest and most prosperous rice plantations situated along the Cooper River. Rice was the main cash crop of the Dean Hall Plantation, and the methods of growing rice used here are fairly typical of eighteenth-century, low-country practices. In the early 1700s, rice was grown by the "inland" method, using water from the reservoir to flood the surrounding rice fields by a system of ditches and trunks. This freshwater reservoir, once used to flood the rice fields, is today's Cypress Gardens swamp. In the late 1700s the new "tidal" method was developed and became highly profitable. This method was used primarily in the low-lying fields immediately adjacent to the Cooper River.

The first plantation home, the Nesbitt House, was built by Sir Alexander Nesbitt of Dean, Scotland, circa 1725. William A. Carson built the second house, Dean Hall, almost one hundred years later. Both houses have since been moved off the plantation. Following the Civil War, Dean Hall fell into neglect and disrepair and remained that way for many years. In 1909, entrepreneur and businessman Benjamin Rufus Kittredge purchased Dean Hall Plantation. Dean Hall provided a winter retreat for his homesick, low-country wife (as well as fine duck hunting for himself and his guests). It is said that the inspiration for Cypress Gardens came to Mr. Kittredge one spring after he saw a brilliant reflection of a red maple in the mirror-like black water of the swamp.

The work began in 1927 when a crew of two hundred men armed with wheelbarrows began the task of clearing the under-growth and building almost three and a half miles of footpaths and nature trails that meander through the swamp and encircle the lake. Numerous small bridges were built linking the islands. Native as well as exotic varieties of plants were selected. Azaleas, spring-blooming ornamental shrubs, and trees were planted close to the swamp's edge so their blossoms would be reflected in its dark waters. Thousands of bulbs were planted everywhere. Mr. Kittredge paid a penny a piece to local boys for each native atamasco lily bulb they could find. As a result, today Cypress Gardens boasts the largest concentration of atamasco lilies in the Southeast. The Cypress Gardens were first opened to the public in 1932 and were donated to the city of Charleston in 1963. The city of Charleston returned the Cypress Gardens to Berkeley County in 1996.

There are many different ways to explore the Cypress Gardens. You can stroll over the footpaths meandering throughout the gardens, observing the **water lilies** and **cattails** growing wherever you look. As you walk, welcome shade is provided by a multitude of tall **willow oaks** (*Quercus phellos*), **pin oaks** (*Quercus palustris*), **black gums** (*Nyssa sylvatica*), **tea olives** (*Osmanthus fragrans*), and **loblolly pines** (*Pinus taeda*). **Weeping willows** (*Salix babylonica*) grow on the edge of the swamp, and magnifi-cent specimens of **bold cypress** (*Taxodium distichum*) thrive in the swamp itself, their images quietly reflected in the still, dark waters. Tannic acid present in the swamp water gives it an extra intense, reflective quality. Yellow jessamine (*Gelsemium sempervirens*) hangs in clusters from the ancient trees. Several smaller, separate gardens are scattered throughout the gardens, just waiting for you to find them: **Azalea Garden, Camellia Garden, Garden of Memories, Woodland Garden, Wedding Garden,** and **Butterfly Garden.** Even a small replica of an inland rice field demonstrating the centuries-old rice-growing methods can be seen here.

The free-standing, walk-through **Butterfly House** features native species of butterflies with all the plants needed to provide nectar for the butterflies and to be a food source for their larvae and caterpillars. The **Freshwater Aquarium** building was recently added. It houses several aquariums displaying freshwater fish, amphibians, and reptiles native to South Carolina. The **Native Tree and Shrub Arboretum** was planted in 1998. It displays trees and shrubs native to the Carolinas and encourages their use in land-scaping.

Departing from the gardens' footpaths are many nature trails leading through the woods. Along these paths you can quietly observe a variety of wildlife species in their natural habitat. Whether you see bald eagles, hawks, ospreys, ducks, herons, egrets, or alliga-tors warming themselves in the sun depends both on your luck and on how quiet you are. If you are even more adventurous, you may explore the gardens on your own, paddling a flat-bottom boat. A guided tour is also available.

The spring peak bloom is quite spectacular, but don't limit your visit just to spring. There is a variety of plants and blossoms to be enjoyed at any time. Maybe the blossoms of the native **atamasco lily** (*Zephyranthes atamasco*) will catch your attention, or the **winter-blooming daphne** (*Daphne odora*) will make you stop and admire. It does not really matter because there is something here to catch your attention at any time.

Nancy Bryan Luce Gardens at Mepkin Abbey

Enjoy azaleas, camellias, dogwoods, and a wide variety of native plants under a canopy of giant, Spanish moss–draped oaks.

Address: P.O. Box 800, Moncks Corner, SC 29461
Directions: From I-26 take exit 199 and go on Alternate US 17. Continue through Moncks Corner and cross the Cooper River. About 0.4 miles past the bridge, make a right turn onto SC 402 and continue for about 2 miles. After crossing the Wadboo Bridge make an immediate right turn onto River Road. After about 5.8 miles the entrance to the abbey will be on your right.
Hours: 9:00 a.m. to 4:30 p.m. daily
Admission fee: no
Wheelchair access: partial
Facilities: Reception Center
Area: 5 acres
Phone: (843) 761-8509

Nestled in the quiet, rolling, pine-wooded countryside along the Cooper River, Mepkin Abbey is a remarkably peaceful place. The site of the present-day abbey and the surrounding acreage used to be a large plantation owned by the first president of the Continental Congress, Henry Laurens. The plantation stayed in family hands for generations. Publisher Henry R. Luce and his wife, Claire B. Luce, eventually purchased the plantation and used it as their summer home. In 1949, a part of the plantation was donated to the order of Cistercian-Trappist Monks, who turned it into a monastery. The gardens of the Mepkin Abbey are named for Nancy Bryan Luce, the wife of Henry R. Luce III.

As you enter the abbey, you will immediately notice the spectacular, ancient Spanish moss–draped **live oaks** lining the driveway. And as you get closer to the gardens you will see even larger and more magnificent live oaks spreading their canopy, in addition to **Southern magnolias, camellias,** and **tea olives.** In spring, blossoms of **dogwoods, rosebuds,** and **wisterias** are breathtaking, but

blooming **azaleas** ultimately steal the show. As you descend the terraces fashioned out of gently rolling hillside, you pass ivy-covered brick walls and pillars as you head toward the ponds and the Cooper River. Feast your eyes on the thousands of azalea blossoms covering the opposite hillside. During our visit, the entire garden was quiet and serene. We enjoyed the sights, sounds, and fragrances and occasionally saw an alligator soaking up the sun by one of the ponds, seemingly oblivious to our presence.

Brookgreen Gardens

The perfect union of nature and art is magnificently displayed at Brookgreen Gardens. Enjoy three hundred manicured acres of America's first public sculpture garden. Over 560 pieces of American nineteenth- and twentieth-century sculpture are set among beautifully landscaped and tranquil gardens, representing the world's largest outdoor collection of American sculpture.

Address: 1931 Brookgreen Gardens Drive, Murrells Inlet, SC 29576
Directions: Take US 17 south from Myrtle Beach. After about 17.5 miles the entrance to the gardens will be on your right, directly across from Huntington Beach State Park.
Hours: 9:30 a.m. to 4:45 p.m. daily
Closed: Christmas
Admission fee: yes
Wheelchair access: yes
Facilities: Welcome Center, Callie & John Rainey Sculpture Pavilion, café, and gift shop
Available: membership, courses, workshops, guided tours
Area: gardens: 300 acres; total property: 9,127 acres
Phone: (843) 237-4218 or (800) 849-1931

In Murrells Inlet, South Carolina, Brookgreen Gardens are the result of the imagination and dreams of Archer and Anna Huntington, who wanted to unite nature and art, thus creating America's first public sculpture garden.

The original property, known as Brookgreen, was settled in the 1700s by the Allston family. In the early nineteenth century, this region was one of the wealthiest in the country because its climate was just about perfect for the cultivation of rice. The next owner, Joshua Ward, ran Brookgreen in the early 1800s as a rice plantation. And when rice was no longer profitable, indigo was grown there. The few subsequent owners used the property for a variety of purposes. The devastation of the colonial economy by the Civil War forced many plantation owners to either sell or abandon their properties. While vacationing in the South Carolina low country in 1929, railroad heir Archer M. Huntington and his wife, Anna Hyatt Hunt-

Brookgreen Gardens
Murrells Inlet

Calhoun Mansion
Charleston

Boone Hall Plantation
Mount Pleasant

Charles Towne Landing
Charleston

Cypress Gardens
Moncks Corner

Hopeland Gardens
Aiken

Magnolia Plantation and Gardens
Charleston

Swan Lake Iris Gardens
Sumter

Summerville Azalea Garden
Summerville

Philip Simmons Garden
Charleston

The Rice Mill, Middleton Place
Charleston

Audubon Swamp Garden
Charleston

ington (one of America's premier sculptors), first heard of Brookgreen Plantation after having read an advertisement for it. In January 1930, the Huntingtons purchased Brookgreen, along with three surrounding rice plantations: Springfield, Laurel Hills, and The Oaks. Their newly acquired property encompassed more than 9,000 acres, stretching from the Atlantic Ocean to the wild rice fields bordering Waccamaw River.

In their master plan for the gardens, the Huntingtons wanted not only to protect and preserve the native flora and variety of ecological habitats, but also to enhance it with additional plantings suitable to the area. Furthermore, they wanted to create an overall design that would showcase Anna Hyatt Huntington's sculptures, as well as the works of other eminent American sculptors. They wanted the formally landscaped gardens to provide a backdrop for many pieces of sculpture. To that end, plants were carefully selected for their color, texture, and size to best showcase each particular sculpture. Among the camellias, azaleas, and magnolias are some of the finest examples of nineteenth- and twentieth-century American figurative sculpture, set among courtyards, tranquil gardens, fountains, ponds, and allées. There are over 560 works by 240 artists, including Daniel Chester French, Frederic Remington, Carl Milles, Laura Gardin Fraser, Charles Parks, August Saint-Gaudens, and, of course, Anna Hyatt Huntington. In 1931, Brookgreen Gardens, Inc.—a Society for Southeastern Flora and Fauna— was organized to administer the gardens.

The gardens proper spread over three hundred manicured acres, planted with more than 2,000 species of indigenous and exotic plants. Visitors can begin their explorations at the Welcome Center by viewing the ten-minute film *Gray Oaks of Mystery,* which describes Brookgreen Gardens: past, present, and future. It will also tell you how to make the most of your visit. If you want to explore on your own, pick up a visitor's guide to the gardens and Wildlife Park. You can also take one of the guided tours.

The **Live Oak Allée** leads you to the large formal garden. Cleverly incorporated into the design, these magnificent **live oak** trees (*Quercus virginiana*), believed to be 250 years old, line the entrance to the original plantation. The **Formal Garden** was planted according to Anna Huntington's butterfly design, with walks laid out in the shape of the outspread wings of a butterfly and the wing segments used as outdoor galleries.

There are other gardens waiting to be explored as well. The **Dogwood Garden** (divided into four quadrants, each with a pool) explodes every spring into a profusion of delicate white blossoms of **dogwood** (*Cornus florida*). The many varieties of dogwood planted here, depending on the cultivars, also add pink or reddish hues according to the colors of their bracts. The **Fountain of the Muses Garden** has a large, rectangular reflecting pool, pergolas, and raised planting beds. There is **Palmetto Garden**, also with a reflecting pool. The **Small Sculpture Gallery**, in a loggia around an interior pool, is enclosed in the manner of a cloister garden. Don't miss the **Old Kitchen Garden**, dating from plantation days, or the **Diana Pool**, the **Arboretum**, the **South Carolina Terrace, Opuntia, Dogwood,** and **Cypress Ponds.**

And what a contrast to the manicured formality of the sculpture gardens is Brookgreen's fifty-acre **Wildlife Park.** There you can explore the **Cypress Aviary, Otter Pond, Fox Glade, Alligator Swamp, White-tailed Deer Savannah,** or **Raptor Aviary.**

What a unique place this is. Beauty is everywhere you look, whether it is gardens, sculptures, or wild nature. It is listed on the National Register of Historic Places and also designated a National Historic Landmark.

Summerville Azalea Garden

Visit here during spring and you will see azalea blossoms every-where you look. Enjoy dogwoods and flowering trees as well.

Address: 104 Civic Center, Summerville, SC 29483
Directions: From I-26 take exit 199A and go south on US 17 Alter-nate for about 2 miles. Make a left turn onto East Richardson Avenue and after 0.1 mile make a right turn onto South Magnolia Street. After about 0.3 miles the garden and parking will be on your right.
Hours: sunrise to sunset daily
Admission fee: no
Wheelchair access: yes
Facilities: none
Area: 10 acres
Phone: (843) 871-6000

In the quiet town of Summerville, the history of the Summerville Azalea Garden goes back to the 1930s. Herbert L. Bailey (who headed Dorchester County's Works Progress Administration), together with Summerville mayor Grange Cuthbert and nursery owner George Segelken, started the project of creating the azalea garden. The Works Progress Administration provided the funds, local residents provided the labor, and nurseryman Segelken donated 30,000 azaleas. The site selected for the garden was locally known as Pike's Hole. Only after clearing the underbrush and draining the swampy land could the planting begin. But soon, beauty could be seen everywhere as azaleas showed off their spring blossoms in profu-sion. As time went by, the garden slid into disrepair. The Summer-ville Preservation Society undertook the revitalization of the garden as its bicentennial project in the early 1970s. The effort was a success and with some additional plantings the garden emerged looking even more beautiful.

Under a canopy of **pines, bold cypress, tupelos, hickories,** and **Southern magnolias, azaleas** seem to thrive. During our spring visit, which coincided with Summerville's "Flowertown Festival," the azaleas were spectacular. Azalea blossoms just about everywhere we looked dazzled us with the spectrum of their colors and hues. In a park-like setting, walkways will guide you over wooden footbridges into various sections of the garden. Walk by the ponds and enjoy the **water lilies** and **irises** along the shoreline. Admire **dogwoods** and other flowering trees in the spring, and blossoms of **camellias** during the winter.

Summerville truly is a Flowertown.

Swan Lake Iris Gardens

See 150 acres of gardens and lakes with a profusion of irises you can rarely see anywhere else. And to top it all off, you can see here all eight known varieties of swans.

Address: P.O. Box 1449, Sumter, SC 29151

Directions: From I-77 take exit 9A and go east on US 378 for about 35 miles until you get to Sumter. Make a right turn onto Alice Drive (SC 120) and go for about 2.6 miles. Make a left turn onto Liberty Street and after about 0.2 miles the garden parking lot will be on your right. From I-95 take exit 135 and go west on US 378 to Sumter. After about 16 miles take Myrtle Beach Highway (SC 763), turn left onto Liberty Street. After about 2.6 miles you will reach the gardens.

Hours: 8 a.m. to sunset daily

Admission fee: no

Wheelchair access: yes

Facilities: none

Area: 150 acres

Phone: (803) 773-3371

Not far east of the state capitol of Columbia, in nice, quiet Sumter, are the ever-popular Swan Lake Iris Gardens. The story of how the gardens began is certainly a fascinating one. Mr. Hamilton Carr Bland was a prominent Sumter businessman and avid gardener. He loved irises, and so in 1927, a huge number of imported irises were planted around his home. Mr. Bland expected to see some spectacular blooms, but despite the meticulous care and advice of experts, the profusion of iris blossoms never happened. Irises just would not bloom. Disappointed by the lack of cooperation from his plants, he ordered that all of his irises be dug up, removed, and dumped in the marshy area of a thirty-acre cypress swamp he had recently purchased. He could not believe his eyes the next spring, when this area was in full bloom. He was delighted by his very successful accident, abandoned his original idea of developing the swamp into a fishing retreat, and instead proceeded with plans to develop this property into a garden. Mr. A.T. Heath was another

Sumter businessman who, in 1938, deeded 120 acres of his neighboring land to the city of Sumter with the stipulation that the land be developed by Mr. Bland as part of the Swan Lake Iris Gardens. Mr. Bland continued to improve the gardens, adding more plantings, and finally deeded the property to the city of Sumter in 1949. Over the years, the city has further improved the gardens.

As you begin to explore the gardens, you will see irises everywhere. Just keep in mind that full bloom is in late spring to early summer. It is said there are six million irises here. Since we were not willing to actually count them, we could not confirm it. We can only state that in all our travels, never have we seen so many irises. Besides **Japanese irises** (known as Kaempferi irises), there are also some Dutch varieties.

And it is not just irises. Enjoy **azaleas, camellias,** and **gardenias** while **cypress, pines, magnolias, oaks,** and **cedars** provide the canopy and shade.

Then there is **Swan Lake**—with its black water—where you can watch swans gliding among **water lilies** and **lotuses**. Swans really are at home here. Longtime residents, they were introduced to the lakes long before the gardens were developed or the irises planted. All of the eight known varieties of swans live here and are a beautiful sight to see. Interpretive markers along the shore will help you identify the swans.

- The **royal white mute swan**, common in Europe, is probably the best known.
- The **trumpeter swan**, native to North America, was named for its trumpetlike call.
- The **whistler swan**, also native to North America, has a white body and black beak.
- The **black-necked swan** is native to South America and the Falklands.
- The **coscoroba swan**, also native to South America and the Falklands, has a white body and orange beak.

- The **whooper swan** is native to Europe and Asia.
- The **bewick swan** is native to Japan.
- The **black Australian swan** has a black body and red beak.

So, when you visit here, you will always face this dilemma: which came first, irises or swans?

Piedmont Region

Spartanburg   Rock Hill
Greenville
Clemson   Union

Newberry   Hartsville
Greenwood   Columbia

Piedmont

Aiken   Orangeburg

Hopeland Gardens

Under a canopy of ancient oaks, right in the city of Aiken, is this delightful garden. From azaleas and dogwoods to roses and camellias, you will be pleasantly surprised.

Address: 149 Dupree Place, P.O. Box 1107, Aiken, SC 29802
Directions: From I-20 take exit 22 and go on US 1 towards Aiken. US 1 eventually becomes York Street. After about 8.4 miles make a right turn onto Richland Avenue and after just one block make a left turn onto Chesterfield Avenue. Continue on Chesterfield Avenue until you reach a fork where you will bear left and continue on Whiskey Road until you make a right turn onto Dupree Place. The garden entrance will be on your left.
Hours: 10:00 a.m. to sunset daily
Admission fee: no
Wheelchair access: partial
Facilities: none
Area: 24 acres
Phone: (803) 642-7630

Hopeland Gardens was once the winter estate of Oliver Iselin and his wife, Hope Goodard Iselin, for whom the gardens are named. Besides her interest in developing gardens on their estate, she was also interested in horses and horseracing. These interests were shared by her wealthy neighbor, Mrs. Dorothy Knox Goodyear Rodgers, of the adjoining estate, called Rye Patch. As the years went by, Mrs. Iselin wanted to preserve her gardens for others to enjoy, so she willed the property to the city of Aiken upon her death in 1970.

There is plenty to see when exploring the gardens. **Giant live oaks** (*Quercus virginiana*) provide welcome shade and the allée of oaks is impressive. And speaking of some really big trees, the **loblolly pines** (*Pinus taeda*) and **deodar cedars** (*Cedrus deodara*), some with multiple trunks, are among the largest we have seen anywhere. In the understory, **azaleas** and **dogwoods** show off in the spring. Enjoy **magnolias** and **crape myrtles**. Garden pathways wind by fountains and reflecting pools; statuary adds still another dimension to the landscape. We enjoyed the **Rose Garden** very

much and are planning to return to see the blossoms in the
Camellia Garden. Still another path follows the shore of the lake
with plenty of **irises** for our eyes to feast on under the towering **bald
cypress** (*Taxodium distichum*). The **Touch and Scent Trail** for the
visually impaired leads to an amphitheater and is lined with interpretive signs in Braille. There is something here to please every
visitor.

Worth Seeing: The **Thoroughbred Racing Hall of Fame** is located
in a restored carriage house and contains trophies and other thoroughbred racing memorabilia.

South Carolina Botanical Garden

Visit South Carolina's first botanical garden. On its 270 acres there are several smaller gardens, displays, and plant collections waiting to be explored and enjoyed.

Address: Clemson University, 102 Garden Trail, Clemson, SC 29634

Directions: From I-85 take exit 19B and go west for about 10 miles on US 76. Make a left turn onto Perimeter Road and after about half a mile the garden entrance will be on your left.

Hours: sunrise to sunset daily

Admission fee: no

Wheelchair access: partial

Facilities: The Wren House (visitor education center), Hayden Conference Center

Available: membership, guided nature walks, horticultural lecture series, educational programs, special events

Area: 270 acres

Phone: (864) 656-3405

Less than two miles east of the Clemson University campus is the South Carolina Botanical Garden. Besides being an important resource garden for Clemson University students, it is also one of South Carolina's most attractive tourist sites, drawing visitors from all across the country.

The garden's beginnings date back to 1958, when Dr. T.L. Senn, Clemson's Professor of Horticulture, founded the Horticultural Gardens of Clemson University. Under his direction work was begun to create the gardens on this forty-four-acre site. It was not an easy task since some portions of this land were heavily eroded and others even contained an abandoned dump. As the years progressed, Dr. Senn's hard work, persistence, and vision paid off as the gardens gradually began to emerge and take shape. Dr. Senn did not just want to display plant collections; he hoped to integrate display, recreation, and nature with conservation, education, and research. Without a doubt, he succeeded. Recognizing its value as a public resource, the Clemson University Board of Trustees decided in 1973 to protect this green space in perpetuity. In 1987, the Clemson University Horticultural Gardens were consolidated with adjoining Clemson University lands and with the Forestry Arboretum to form the 270-acre Clemson University Botanical Garden. It was renamed in 1992 as South Carolina Botanical Garden, the state's first botanical garden. Looking back at it all, it is hard to believe that a small camellia collection planted in 1958 on a reclaimed landfill site has grown into a major public garden.

This beautiful garden is certainly a place to relax and to enjoy the plant collections, but it is also a place to learn. The garden serves as an interdisciplinary resource center for students of Clemson University studying horticulture, landscape design, forestry, and natural sciences. It also serves as an outdoor classroom for a wide variety of interest groups from school children to senior citizens, teaching them about plants, gardening, and conservation. There is also ongoing research focusing on many areas such as the adaptability of plants, environmental problems, the value of plants for food, and recombinant gene research, just to name a few. The mission statement of the South Carolina Botanical Garden summarizes it best: "The mission of the South Carolina Botanical Garden is to serve as an interdisciplinary public garden whose focus is research and education in the areas of botanical and cultural conservation and the environment."

With several smaller gardens and many plantings and collections, there is so much to see here. As you enter the garden you cannot miss the bright red caboose, a gift from the Southern Railway Company and a prominent landmark since 1973. This area has been designated as the **Class of '39 Caboose Garden** for the university class that has strongly supported the development of the Botanical Garden. The red caboose also serves as a meeting place for tour groups, classes, and guided nature walks. The **T.L. Senn Horticultural Garden** that was dedicated in honor of its founder on June 8, 1991, surrounds the Caboose Garden. This is the garden's original forty-four-acre tract of land. The **Camellia Garden** represents the first planting at the garden. From modest beginnings, through steady additions of new specimens, it now contains more than three hundred varieties of camellias. Their blossoms are waiting to be admired from fall to spring. The **Flower Display Garden** covers two acres and the color spectrum of its annuals and perennials changes with the seasons.

Visit the **L.O. Van Blaricom Xeriscape Garden** and learn more about water conservation and the xeriscape concept. A stroll through this garden clearly demonstrates that a garden can be lush-looking even with water usage reduced by up to eighty percent. Proper xeriscape methods are not limited to water conservation only, but also include landscape designs and plant selections that result in a low-maintenance garden that also looks great. The need for pesticide application is almost eliminated, as is its potential harm to the environment. In addition to water, you are also saving time, effort, and money. The **Roland Schoenike Arboretum** contains a diverse collection of more than one thousand woody plants of historic or commercial importance to the horticulture and forestry of this region. Many rare species can be found here and since most of the collection is fully mature now, it creates a perfect outdoor classroom.

More than 350 varieties of **hostas** are featured in the **Charles and Betty Cruickshank Hosta Garden**. Hostas (Plantain lily), native to China and Japan, are popular, shade-loving, frost-hardy perennials. They are low-growing, clump-forming, and are grown mostly for their attractive, large and ribbed foliage. You can admire the variety of their sizes, colors, and textures from spring to fall. The **Jack Miller Memorial Conifer Garden** displays **conifers** (cone-bearing plants), and the **dwarf conifer** collection contains more than fifty species and cultivars. True dwarf conifers never become very large and usually grow very slowly. Complementary plantings of **irises, daffodils**, and a variety of other perennials brighten the garden with a splash of color. The **Bernice Lark Wildflower Meadow** and **Piedmont Prairie Garden** feature acres of **wildflowers** and **ornamental grasses**. Your eyes can feast not only on a colorful variety of wildflowers but also on butterflies, humming-birds, and other wildlife they attract.

The nearby **Lake and Hills Garden Club Butterfly Garden** provides even more butterfly-nurturing environment. Plants here please our eyes and provide everything needed for the life cycle of the butterfly. Adult butterflies need nectar from flowering plants as a food source, but the plant-food sources for caterpillars are not necessarily the same as those used by adult butterflies as a source of nectar. Different species of butterflies prefer different species of flowers. Most species of butterflies will lay eggs only on one species of plant. Once the eggs hatch, the larvae begin to feed on the host plant. Are you beginning to see what it takes to create a butterfly habitat? Leaves of some plants serve as food for the caterpillars, blossoms of other plants provide the nectar for adult butterflies, while butterfly bushes and small trees surrounding the garden provide the needed windbreak. Even the shallow bank of a nearby pond is important, providing a place where the butterflies obtain water and minerals from the soil. And as you enjoy the flowers and beautiful butterflies, the interpretive signs will enlighten you about the butterfly habitat and plants needed at various stages of the life cycle of the butterfly.

As you explore the garden, don't miss the **Azalea and Rhodo-dendron Collection** or the **Japanese Maple Collection**. The **Therapeutic Horticulture Garden** opens itself to visitors with physical challenges. Raised beds and wide walks that easily accommodate wheelchairs make a visit here readily accessible. A gazebo provides a quiet, shady area to rest and relax. The **Pioneer Herb Garden** and the nearby Pioneer Cabins and Grist Mill are at the beginning of the **Braille Trail**. Plants are meant to be touched and smelled along this trail. Guide ropes and interpretive Braille signs lead vision-impaired visitors from the Pioneer Garden through the **Belser Nature Trail**, which features many species of **wildflowers**, **ferns**, and **bog plants**. **Magnolia Lane**, adjoining the Garden's Loop Road, is a unique and impressive collection of hundreds of **magnolia** specimens. The quiet **Meditation Garden**, with its moss-covered gazebo, is the place to rest, relax, and reflect while watching the waterfall and small reflecting pool.

Several hiking and birdwatching trails wind through the garden as well. What else could one ask for—a beautiful garden in which to relax, enjoy, and learn.

Worth Seeing: Visit the **Hanover House**, originally built in 1716 by French Huguenot Paul de St. Julien in Berkeley County of the South Carolina low country. By marriage of Paul de St. Julien's eldest daughter, the house passed from the St. Julien family to the Ravenel family, in whose possession it remained for almost 140 years. But subsequent years were not kind to the house. In the early 1900s the house was in great disrepair—almost in ruins—and by the early 1940s was completely dilapidated and abandoned. And as if that were not enough, this entire area was to be flooded by the South Carolina Public Service Authority's Santee-Cooper Hydroelectric

Project, designed to create Lake Moultrie. Luckily, the house was recognized for its historical and architectural values and the decision was made to save it. The search for a new location began. That new location turned out to be Clemson College, 250 miles north of the house's original site.

The relocation work began in 1941. After detailed drawings and photographs were made, every brick, beam, and board was carefully labeled to enable exact reassembly on the new site, Clemson's central campus. Then the slow process of restoration began. Furnishings were added to interpret the period from 1700 to 1750. Finally, in June 1962, the Hanover House was officially opened as a museum. In order to allow for the new student activity center, the house was moved to the South Carolina Botanical Garden in July 1994. This house has survived almost three centuries and two relocations. Let's hope it will stay here for a very long time. Hanover House is listed on the National Register of Historic Places. Tours of the house are offered to visitors from 10:00 a.m. to 5:00 p.m. on Saturdays and from 2:00 p.m. to 5:00 p.m. on Sundays.

Boylston Gardens

The gardens and grounds of this complex symbolize the beauty of South Carolina. From fountains and showy blossoms to quiet secluded gardens, it's all right here in Columbia.

Address: Governor's Mansion, 800 Richland Street, Columbia, SC 29201
Directions: From I-20 take exit 64A and go east on I-26 until it becomes Elmwood Avenue. After about 3.5 miles make a right turn onto Lincoln Street. The entrance to the gardens is at the corner of Lincoln and Richland Streets.
Hours: 9:30 a.m. to 4:30 p.m. Monday to Friday
Admission fee: no
Wheelchair access: yes
Facilities: none
Area: 9 acres
Phone: (803) 737-1710

Boylston Gardens is a part of Governor's Green, a nine-acre, three-mansion complex surrounded by massive and elaborate fencing. The Caldwell-Boylston House was built in 1830, the Lace House in 1854, and the Governor's Mansion in 1855. The Governor's Mansion was built by the Arsenal Military Academy to house their officers. In 1868, Governor James L. Orr recommended that the building, situated on grounds the state already owned, be used as the executive mansion. The mansion has been occupied continuously since 1879, and Robert K. Scott became the first South Carolina governor to live there. The elaborate, decorative ironwork of the Lace House makes it appear as if trimmed in lace. Even the gate and surrounding wrought-iron fence have the same "lacy" effect. And make certain you do not miss seeing the unusually beautiful pair of palmetto-design iron gates guarding the entry into the enclosed patio garden on the south side of the mansion.

One can encounter unexpected variety in this nine-acre complex, including a **rose garden**, fountains, and **boxwood hedges**. Tree-lined pathways lead to quiet, secluded gardens and parklike areas with a wide expanse of lawn under **live oak** trees and **Southern**

magnolias. During our spring visit we found blossoming **azaleas** and **dogwoods** and the most magnificent specimens of **deodar cedar** (*Cedrus deodara*), **white cedar** (*Thuja occidentalis*), and **tulip tree** (*Liriodendron tulipifera*) we have seen anywhere. The largest **crape myrtle** in the state of South Carolina is located here as well.

Memorial Garden

This small and intimate walled garden, adjacent to the
Governor's Mansion complex, is spectacular in spring.

Address: Garden Club of South Carolina, c/o Mrs. Herbert A.
Wood, 1107 Jessamine Street, Cayce, SC 29033
Directions: From I-20 take exit 64A and go east on I-26 until it
becomes Elmwood Avenue. After about 3.5 miles make a right
turn onto Lincoln Street. The garden is located at 1919 Lincoln
Street, with entry near the corner of Lincoln and Calhoun Streets.
Hours: 1:00 p.m. to 5:00 p.m., Sunday, or by appointment
Admission fee: no
Wheelchair access: yes
Facilities: none
Area: ¼ acre
Phone: (803) 796-6446

In 1945, the Garden Club of South Carolina decided to establish
the Memorial Garden "to honor and perpetuate the memory of
all South Carolinians who served in World War II." A search
committee was formed to look for a property that would be suitable
and affordable. This was not an easy task and eventually Sarah Smith
Boylston, a search committee member, donated a portion of her own
garden. Renowned Charleston landscape architect Loutrel W. Briggs
designed the master plan for the garden and donated it to the
Garden Club of South Carolina. Funding was obtained from donations of individuals, businesses, and even the city of Columbia and
the South Carolina State Legislature. The formal opening of the
garden was in 1946, and after its completion as designed, the dedica-
tion was held in April 1957. This garden was the first Memorial
Garden established by any state garden club after World War II.

A heavy, wrought-iron double gate and gatehouse guard the
entry into this walled garden. The center lawn is bordered with
boxwood and plantings of **azaleas, dogwoods, star magnolias,**
camellias, sasanquas, crape myrtles, tea olives, and **loquats.**
There is a tall hedge of **Carolina cherries** as well as **ivy, hollies,** and
a variety of **evergreens.** A wrought-iron trellis is covered with

yellow jessamine. A statue of St. Francis of Assisi shares space with four statues representing each of the seasons. You will find a visit here very tranquil.

Riverbanks Botanical Garden

This young botanical garden is on seventy acres just outside of Columbia. Besides its centerpiece Walled Garden, there are several smaller gardens to enjoy.

Address: Hwy. 126 and Greystone Boulevard, Columbia, SC 29202
Directions: From I-20 take exit 64A and go east on I-126 until the
    Greystone Boulevard exit. Follow signs. In just about 0.2 miles
    you will come to the garden's parking lot.
Hours: 9:00 a.m. to 4:00 p.m. daily; closed Thanksgiving and
    Christmas
Admission fee: yes
Wheelchair access: yes
Facilities: Visitors Center, gift shops, snack bars, and café
Available: membership, educational programs, classes, lectures
Area: entire complex: 170 acres; Botanical Garden: 70 acres
Phone: (803) 779-8717

Lower Saluda River runs through the 170-acre Riverbanks complex, dividing it into the Zoological Park on one side and the Botanical Garden on the other, joined by a bridge that spans the river. Situated on the river's west bank, the seventy-acre Riverbanks Botanical Garden site offers breathtaking and spectacular scenic river views. The garden site covers three distinct topographic features: a floodplain valley rises through valley slopes to the uplands above. Preceded by years of planning, this young garden opened to the public in the summer of 1995.

The **Entry Court Garden** just in front of the Visitors Center will give you the first hint that you are in for a treat. Walk through the Visitors Center and you will enter the **Walled Garden** that is unquestionably the true centerpiece of the Riverbanks Botanical Garden. Surrounded by an eight-foot-tall brick wall, it contains several smaller individual gardens and plantings that offer their colors, textures, and scents to be admired. Water defines the central axis of the Walled Garden, flowing down the three-hundred-foot-long canal with cascades and pinwheel fountains. Brick-paved walkways lead you to the periphery of the garden, where you will discover

and enjoy additional
smaller gardens and
plantings of trees,
shrubbery, and vines.
There is so much to
see. And if you enjoy
flowering vines, you
are in for a treat.

During our visit
the profusion of
orange/pink blossoms
of the **Chinese
trumpet creeper**
(*Campsis grandiflora*) was
just magnificent and so were the delicate, salmon-colored blossoms
of another trumpet creeper (*Campsis radicans*). Colors and fragrances
vary with the seasons. Seasonal plantings add splashes of color
throughout the year. In early spring over fifty thousand bulbs flower
throughout the garden, and the sight of **tulips** and **daffodils** is just
spectacular. During the summer a wide variety of annuals add their
colors, followed in fall and on into the winter by remarkable combi-
nations of **pansies, asters,** bulbs, and winter green vegetables.

In the **Knot Garden** (built around a traditional knot design
where hedges seem to be intertwined) you will find many culinary
and fragrant **herbs**. Over five hundred varieties of **daylilies** flower in
the **Daylily Garden** and there are the **Art Garden, Fountain
Garden,** and **Midnight Garden** waiting to be enjoyed. In the **Rose
Garden,** located just outside of the Walled Garden, one finds a
profusion of colors and scents of many varieties of **roses,** especially
old roses. The collection of **noisettes** is quite impressive and is
considered one of the largest in the world. Of other **old roses, teas**
and **Chinas** are also well represented. Sit on a bench, admire the
roses, or rest and relax before starting down the **Woodlands Walk**.

This young garden is beautiful now; it will be spectacular as it
matures.

Worth Seeing: **Riverbanks Zoo.** Opened to the public in 1974, this
nationally acclaimed, award-winning zoological park was named as
one of the ten great zoos in the United States and is dedicated to the

conservation of our earth's fauna and flora. More than two thousand animals thrive in recreated natural habitats, where psychological barriers (such as water, moats, and light) replace bars and cages.

Saluda Mill Ruins. Nestled in the wooded area just above the rushing river and near the site of the old cotton mill ruins is the recently opened **Saluda Factory Interpretive Center**. Located in a log cabin, the center features artifacts and drawings found at the site and even includes an outdoor classroom for lectures and classes. In addition to its beauty, this site is also of considerable historical significance. It was the site of the Saluda Manufacturing Company, one of the first water-powered textile factories in South Carolina. And it was here that General Sherman and his troops crossed the river to enter and burn the city of Columbia during the Civil War.

Robert Mills House

A parklike setting surrounds this 1800s mansion. Enjoy the smaller gardens closer to the house.

Address: 1616 Blanding Street, Columbia, SC 29201
Directions: From I-20 take exit 64A and go east on I-26 until it
   becomes Elmwood Avenue. After about 4.5 miles make a right
   turn onto Assembly Street, go four blocks and make a left turn
   onto Blanding Street.
Hours: grounds: sunrise to sunset daily; house: 10:15 a.m. to 3:15
   p.m. Tuesday to Saturday; 1:15 p.m. to 4:15 p.m. Sunday.
Admission fee: grounds, no; house, yes
Wheelchair access: grounds, yes
Facilities: none
Area: 4 acres
Phone: (803) 252-1770

This mansion is one of the few residences designed by South
Carolina's most famous architect, Robert Mills. A native of
Charleston, Mills was the Federal Architect of the United
States under seven presidents. He designed the Washington Monument, the U.S. Treasury Building, the Old Patent Office, and a host
of other structures. Mills designed this house in 1823 for Ainsley
Hall, a wealthy Columbia merchant. Hall died before the house was
completed, saddling his wife with tremendous debt. She was forced
to sell the house in order to cover the debt.

The Presbyterian Theological Seminary purchased the house in
1831 and used it for almost one hundred years. The carriage house
on the grounds of the seminary served as a chapel for the students,
and President Woodrow Wilson's father, who was on the faculty,
used to preach there. Woodrow Wilson later remembered these
services as the most important in his life. Later on, the property was
used by Winthrop College and by Columbia Bible College. In the
early 1960s the house was threatened with demolition and was saved
only by the heroic efforts of preservationists of the Historic
Columbia Foundation and Richland County Historic Preservation
Commission. The outbuildings were rebuilt and the house was

painstakingly restored and furnished as a decorative arts museum.

The grounds were authentically restored to the appearance appropriate for homes of the early 1800s. The landscape in front of the house is parklike with an expanse of green lawn under large **Southern magnolias, live oaks**, and **hickories**. Do not miss the **Founder's Garden**.

Behind the house is a **boxwood** garden with a small statuary, boxwood maze, and plantings of **roses**. Enjoy beautiful specimens of **crape myrtle**. A visit to this National Historic Landmark is very peaceful and relaxing.

Worth Seeing: Take a tour of this 1823 house, one of the few private residences designed by Robert Mills that is still standing. This mansion was designed in Federal/Greek revival style, with its ionic column porch, symmetrical doorways, Venetian windows, and curved walls. Richly decorated with ceiling ornamentation, crystal chandeliers, and marble mantels, right down to sterling silver doorknobs, the house is furnished with a fine collection of early nineteenth-century French Empire, English Regency, and American Federal furniture.

The Horseshoe at the University of South Carolina

Stroll the historic original campus of the University of South Carolina under the welcoming shade of the majestic oaks. There are five gardens to enjoy here.

Address: Visitor Center – Carolina Plaza, 937 Assembly Street, Columbia, SC 29201

Directions: From I-20 take exit 64A and go east on I-26 until it becomes Elmwood Avenue. After about 4.5 miles make a right turn onto Assembly Street. Continue on Assembly Street until you make a left turn onto Pendleton Street. After two blocks make a right turn onto Sumter Street. The Horseshoe is right there; you can't miss it.

Hours: sunrise to sunset daily

Admission fee: no

Wheelchair access: yes

Facilities: none

Area: 4 city blocks

Phone: (803) 777-8161

Under a canopy of majestic oaks, the Horseshoe is the original campus of the University of South Carolina and is its historical and sentimental heart. Chartered in 1801 as South Carolina College, most of its buildings were constructed between 1805 and 1855. The buildings reflect the Federal style of architecture, quite fashionable at that time. The architecture of South Carolina College was greatly influenced by Robert Mills, the nation's first federal architect, who was instrumental in the design of the South Caroliniana Library, Rutledge College, and Maxcy Monument, named for the first president of the college, Jonathan Maxcy. Out of eleven buildings standing on the Horseshoe, ten of them were built during the early to mid-1800s. Only the McKissick Museum was constructed at a later date (in 1940).

South Carolina College was a highly respected institution with a renowned faculty. Classes were suspended during the Civil War, after almost the entire student body enlisted in the Army of the Confederacy. During those turbulent years fate was kind to the Horseshoe. It survived the burning of Columbia by Sherman's army. The college buildings were used as a hospital, housing for prisoners and refugees, and state and federal offices. After the Civil War, South Carolina College was renamed University of South Carolina and grew beyond its original campus. The Horseshoe quadrangle began to fall into a state of neglect and disrepair. An extensive program of renovations in the 1970s was aimed at restoring all these historic structures to their 1850s appearance. And what a success it was. In 1983, the restoration project received the Preservation Award for Public Building Renovation from the Historic Columbia Foundation. The Horseshoe is listed on the National Register of Historic Places.

The Horseshoe Gardens were added during the restoration of the old campus in the 1970s. The gardens are lovely and intimate. Look for them in between or behind the beautiful, historic buildings along the edge of the Horseshoe.

The **Rose Garden at Lieber** is tucked in between Lieber College and Pinckney College. Brick paths will lead you through various sections of the garden while high brick walls shelter the **roses** and provide welcome privacy. Quiet nooks with benches invite you to sit down, relax, enjoy the roses or just contemplate. The garden was funded by contributions from the Columbia Garden Club and honors deceased garden club members. The **President's House Garden**, located directly behind the President's House, is not open to the public but one may view it from the gate. Of note is the beautiful **crape myrtle**, over three stories tall and believed to be more than 150 years old. It is not only the largest crape myrtle around the Horseshoe but one of the largest in South Carolina. South of McKissick Museum and adjacent to Rutledge College, the **Sundial Garden** was just recently restored by Omicron Delta Kappa in honor of its members and alumni. In the **McCutchen House Garden**, nestled between McCutchen House and DeSaussure College, you can enjoy **azaleas, camellias,** and **Bradford pear trees**, as well as large crape myrtles. Borders planted with seasonal annuals provide a splash of color. The **Caroliniana Garden**, situated behind South Caroliniana Library, was restored mainly through the efforts of Mrs. Edmund Taylor, former president of the University of South Caroliniana Society. Enjoy plantings of **azaleas, gardenias, nand-**

inas, and **sasanquas**, as well as several varieties of **ilex**, which thrive under **magnolias** and **Japanese maples**. An impressive, three-tiered fountain, dedicated to the Carolina Patriots who fought in the American Revolution, graces the garden.

It is hard to believe this area is part of a busy campus. We found our visit here enjoyable, and our walks through the serene and dignified Horseshoe made us feel as if we were stepping back in time.

Japanese Garden of Furman University

A small, Japanese garden right on the university campus.

Address: 3300 Poinsett Highway, Greenville, SC 29613
Directions: From I-85 take exit 46 and go north on Augusta Road (US 25 Bus) all the way through Greenville until it (US 25 Bus) becomes Poinsett Highway. Watch for signs; the entrance to the campus will be on your right. The garden is on the university campus.
Hours: sunrise to sunset daily
Admission fee: no
Wheelchair access: partial
Facilities: none
Area: 2 acres
Phone: (864) 294-2179 or (864) 294-2000

I t is hard to believe that this garden was once an unsightly, two-acre swamp at the north end of the lake. The garden was laid out and planted in 1963, with ponds, palisade paths, and small bridges incorporated into the design.

Located by the lake at the edge of the busy campus, the garden offers a place for quiet reflection. Walk the paths, cross the footbridges, and enjoy the colors and textures. In spring, a spectrum of colors is provided not just by **azaleas** and **dogwoods** but also by blossoms of **weeping Higan cherry** (*Prunus subhirtella*), **redbud crabapple** (*Malus sieboldii*), and **apple trees** (*Malus pumila*). **Bald cypress, pines,** and **gums** provide the shade as you explore. We enjoyed nice specimens of **Japanese maple** (*Acer palmatum*), **Amur maple** (*Acer ginnala*), **China fir** (*Cunninghamia lanceolata*), and **Japanese cedar** (*Cryptomeria japonica*). We found this tranquil garden quite enjoyable.

Park Seed Company Trial and Display Garden

This famous garden showcases summer annuals, bulbs, vegetables, herbs, and roses. It is the largest trial garden for annuals in the Southeast.

Address: 1 Parkton Avenue, Greenwood, SC 29647

Directions: From I-26 take exit 54 and go south on SC 72 into Greenwood. SC 72 becomes SC 72/US 221. Make a right turn onto Reynolds Avenue (SC 254) and go for about 6 miles. The garden will be on your left.

Hours: sunrise to sunset daily

Fee: no

Wheelchair access: yes

Facilities: Park Seed Company Store

Area: 9 acres

Phone: (864) 223-7333 or (864) 223-8555

Just six miles north of Greenwood, the George W. Park Seed Company's famous trial gardens constitute the largest trial garden for annuals in the Southeast. In 1868, George W. Park, who was just sixteen years old at the time, started a mail-order business, using the seeds he had obtained from his own garden. He designed his own eight-page catalogue, his business became a success, and the rest is history. But George W. Park wanted to be more knowledgeable about the seeds he was selling. So in 1882, with money he had earned from his business, he enrolled in Michigan State University and completed a degree in horticulture. He returned to his business in Pennsylvania, only to find that its climate was not conducive to growing a variety of plants. After moving to Greenwood, South

Carolina, however, his business really took off and prospered. George W. Park died in 1935, but his family continued to run the business. Today Park Seed Company is still owned and operated by members of the Park family.

Several demonstration and test gardens surround the Park Seed nine-acre facility, five of which are open to the public. And what a profusion of blossoms, colors, and textures. Feast your eyes on more than 1,500 **summer annuals, bulbs, vegetables, herbs,** and **roses.** Summer annuals are at their peak during the second half of June and that, without question, is a sight not to be missed.

Kalmia Gardens of Coker College

The profusion of blossoming mountain laurels will certainly fascinate you. Enjoy azaleas and camellias too.

Address: 1624 West Carolina Avenue, Hartsville, SC 29550
Directions: From I-20 take exit 116 and go on US 15 for about 20
   miles to downtown Hartsville. From there continue west on SC
   Business 151 (Carolina Avenue). You will reach the gardens after
   about 2.6 miles. From I-95 take exit 164 and go west on Rt. 52
   for about 7.3 miles until you reach SC 151 leading to Hartsville.
   Continue on SC 151 until you reach fork in the road, where you
   bear right to SC 151 Business. After about 4 additional miles
   turn left at traffic light in downtown Hartsville on Carolina
   Avenue. Continue on Carolina Avenue for about 2.7 miles and
   garden entrance will be on your right.
Hours: sunrise to sunset daily
Admission fee: no
Wheelchair access: partial
Facilities: none
Area: 30 acres
Phone: (843) 383-8145 or (843) 383-8000

The land on which the gardens are located was originally part
of two hundred acres granted to Benjamin Davis by King
George III in 1772. During subsequent years the land was
subdivided and changed hands several times. In 1817, Thomas
Edwards Hart, for whom Hartsville is named, acquired the property
and around 1820 he built his house on the bluff overlooking the
Black Creek. He established a prosperous plantation on over 1,200
acres that produced mainly cotton and tobacco. After the Civil War
and through the turn of the century, the property again changed
hands several times and eventually fell into neglect and disrepair. Dr.
William Chambers Coker, head of the Botany Department at the
University of North Carolina at Chapel Hill, was interested in the
area surrounding the Thomas Hart House. This acreage was known
as "Laurel Land" because of the profusion of mountain laurels
growing among the bluffs along Black Creek. He acquired this over-

grown property in 1931 and gave it to his sister-in-law, May Roper Coker. An avid gardener, she quickly started to transform this waste woodland and swampland into a garden paradise. Many people openly wondered whether her efforts would succeed. What needed to be accomplished here was certainly not a small task. Trails leading down the bluffs had to be carved, a pond fed by an artesian well was dug, and plantings of camellias, azaleas, wisteria, and other exotic plants were added along the trails.

Working tirelessly, she succeeded, overcoming doubts, skepticism, and even the Great Depression. She decided to call the gardens Kalmia Gardens, named for the mountain laurel (*Kalmia latifolia*) growing in abundance there. The Kalmia Gardens were open to the public free of charge in 1935. In 1965, May Roper Coker donated the gardens to Coker College as a memorial to her late husband, David Robert Coker. Today, in addition to their beauty, the Kalmia Gardens also serve as an outdoor classroom, offering a variety of educational programs for students and the public alike. As summarized by their mission statement: "The mission of Kalmia Gardens of Coker College is to serve as a botanical garden and outdoor classroom where plants and animals can be observed in their environment. To the extent possible, the garden shall be maintained and developed for the benefit, education, and enjoyment of the general public where people may walk, watch, listen, and feel as seasonal changes enhance its natural beauty."

We timed our visit just right and were rewarded with the spectacular sight of blooming mountain laurels just about everywhere we looked. After picking up a self-guided map of the gardens, first we wanted to see the laurels; that's why we came here. There is a sixty-foot drop in elevation from the house to the Black Creek and from the trails leading down the bluff one can admire the surrounding beauty. It really seems that laurels drape the bluffs in a white veil. There are several trails to explore – **Bluff Trail, Rhododendron Trail, Black Creek Trail, Camellia Trail, Bog Garden Trail, Kalmia Loop,** and **Boardwalk** just to name a few. The benches along the trails welcome you to sit down for a while to rest, enjoy the scenery, or just contemplate. There are more than just **mountain laurels**. Enjoy **camellias, azaleas,** and **dogwoods** under a canopy of towering **pines, oaks,** and **cedars**.

And there is still more to see. Do not miss the **Daylily Collec-**

tion, Herb Garden, Bog Garden, Sensory Garden, Rhododendron Garden, Kalmia Varieties Collection, and Purple Garden.
A remarkably large **American beech tree** (*Fagus grandifolia*) next to
the Capt. Thomas Edwards Hart House is one of the largest we have
seen.

Our visit here was an unexpectedly pleasurable surprise. We
expected to see mountain laurels and we certainly did, plus much,
much more.

Wells Japanese Garden

What a pleasantly unexpected find. A small, Japanese garden just steps away from Newberry's historic downtown. You will love the garden and you will most likely enjoy it all by yourself.

Address: Newberry Chamber of Commerce, P.O. Box 396, Newberry, SC 29108

Directions: From I-26 take exit 72 and go south on SC 121 to Newberry. CS 121 will lead you to College Street. Continue on College Street past Newberry College. Make a left turn onto Spears Street, go for one block and make a right turn onto Lindsey Street. The garden will be on your left.

Hours: 7:00 a.m. to 7:00 p.m. daily

Admission fee: no

Wheelchair access: partial

Facilities: none

Area: ¾ acre

Phone: (803) 276-4274

Just a step away from Newberry's historic downtown is Wells Japanese Garden. It was conceived by the Henry B. Wells family and built according to a design by Fulmer Wells in 1930 as their private garden of exotic plants set among ponds connected by wooden bridges. Fulmer Wells deeded the garden to the city of Newberry in 1971. In 1984, the Newberry County Council of Garden Clubs took over the maintenance of this somewhat neglected garden. The Council set about restoring the garden to its former beauty—no easy task, to say the least. The restoration involved a major clean-up, including removing undesirable plants, cleaning the ponds, tagging existing plants, and adding new plants. Countless hours of hard work by local garden clubs and volunteers, as well as generous donations by local citizens and businesses, were the keys to success. And all of this under the guidance of Dr. Gordon Halfacre, horticulturist and landscape architect from Clemson University, who designed a master plan for the restoration and beautification of the garden.

Our visit was totally enjoyable and as an added benefit we had the garden completely to ourselves since no one else was around. If you visit in the spring, **azaleas** and **dogwoods** will show off their blossoms. Since we were visiting during early summer we saw **lotuses** blossoming in the ponds. We found the blossoms of the **sacred lotus** (*Nelumbium nucifera*) especially spectacular. And as you explore the garden, pathways will lead you over the wooden foot-bridges, by the groves of **bamboo**, under the **bald cypress** with its knees popping out of the ground. Now you begin to appreciate what Newberry County Garden Clubs accomplished here.

Edisto Memorial Gardens

Enjoy azaleas, dogwoods, and wisteria under a canopy of tall, bald cypress and oaks on 150 acres along the North Edisto River. You will also find a beautiful rose garden and much more.

Address: Orangeburg Chamber of Commerce, 250 John C. Calhoun Drive, Orangeburg, SC 29116

Directions: From I-26 take exit 149 and go on SC 33 into Orangeburg. After about 5.3 miles, just before SC 33 joins US 301, you will see the gardens on your right.

Hours: sunrise to sunset daily

Admission fee: no

Wheelchair access: yes

Facilities: none

Area: 150 acres

Phone: (803) 534-6821 or (803) 533-6020

On the outskirts of Orangeburg, the Edisto Memorial Gardens are located along the North Edisto River. They were created from a dismal, swampy area along the riverbank, where five acres of azaleas were planted in the early 1920s. Originally called Edisto Gardens, this city park just kept expanding. In 1950, a large fountain was added as a memorial to the soldiers who died in World Wars I and II and the Korean and Vietnam Wars. In 1951, rose gardens were added, with plantings of more than five thousand roses of more than two hundred varieties. Designated as an All-American Rose Selection display garden, it is one of twenty-three test sites in the United States that is used to determine the hardiness of a variety of roses planted in different regions of the country. So, from its humble beginnings, Edisto Memorial Gardens became so popular that more than four hundred thousand visitors come each year to admire its beauty.

Start your visit by picking up a self-guided tour booklet at the Orangeburg County Chamber of Commerce (803-534-6821) or the Orangeburg Arts Center River Pavilion (803-536-4073) located near the gardens. That way you will not miss any section of the gardens. During the spring, blossoms of **azaleas** and **dogwoods** growing beneath towering **bald cypress trees** and **oaks** are just breathtaking. The **bald cypress** (*Taxodium distichum*) growing near the lake are majestic. And when you add blossoms of **wisteria, magnolias,** and **roses,** you can see the whole palette of colors. During our visit, the rose garden looked spectacular. Roses, roses everywhere, no matter which way you turned. We really enjoyed a trellis with beautiful, climbing

Lady Banksia roses (*Rosa banksiae*) showcasing their yellow blossoms against the blue skies. All the roses are well labeled, which makes their identification easy. Explore the nature trail and a garden for the blind. And if you need a little rest after all that exploring, there is a gazebo and a picnic area to relax in. Do not miss the latest addition: the six-acre Horne Wetlands Park. It is accessible by a 2,700-foot boardwalk, from which visitors can take a close-up look at the plants and wildlife indigenous to this wetland area. There is even a boat dock for those who want to explore the Edisto River by canoe. The Edisto is the longest flowing blackwater river in the world.

Glencairn Garden

This parklike garden right in the middle of the city of Rock Hill offers spectacular displays when the azaleas and flowering trees are in the peak of their bloom.

Address: P.O. Box 11706, 155 Johnston Street, Rock Hill, SC
   29731
Directions: From I-77 take exit 82B and go west on Cherry Road
   for about 3.2 miles. Make a left turn onto Charlotte Avenue and
   after about 0.8 miles make another left turn onto Edgemont
   Avenue. The garden entrance and parking will be on your right.
Hours: sunrise to sunset daily
Admission fee: no
Wheelchair access: yes
Facilities: none
Area: 7.5 acres
Phone: (803) 329-5620

In 1928, Dr. David A. Bigger and his wife, Hazel, pursuing a hobby of theirs, started to create their own private garden. As the years went by and the beauty of the garden became more and more evident, the Biggers wanted to ensure that future generations would share the enjoyment of this beautiful garden they were so proud of. So in 1958, thirty years after having started the garden, Hazel M. Bigger donated the property to the city of Rock Hill and the city continued to further develop the garden.

Thousands of **azaleas** of many varieties will immediately catch your attention if you visit during spring. It is a quiet, parklike garden with sculptured, terraced lawns, flower beds, brick borders, **boxwood hedges,** and winding pathways. Cascading fountains flow into the reflecting pool with **water lilies** and goldfish. Blossoms of **dogwoods, redbuds,** and **crape myrtles** reflect in the lily pond while **oaks, pines, cedars,** and **bald cypress** provide the shade. This is a perfect place to just sit down, contemplate, and enjoy.

Hatcher Gardens

You will find seven acres of gardens, ponds, wildflowers, and native plants to be enjoyed right here in Spartanburg.

Address: Spartanburg County Foundation, 320 East Main Street, Spartanburg, SC 29302

Directions: From I-26 take exit 22 and go east towards Spartanburg on SC 296 (Reidville Road). After about 1.9 miles the entrance to the gardens will be on your left at 820 Reidville Road.

Hours: 9:00 a.m. to sunset daily

Admission fee: no

Wheelchair access: partial

Facilities: none

Area: 7 acres

Phone: (803) 582-2776

It all started in 1969, when Harold Hatcher purchased an abandoned cotton field, overgrown with weeds, as a place he wanted to retire. His vision was to transform this sorry sight into a beautiful garden full of flowers, trees, and plants, teeming with native birds and wildlife, where people could come and learn about the preservation of an environment, as well as horticulture and landscaping. As thousands of plants were planted, this property was transformed into the gardens Mr. Hatcher had visualized. But he was also aware of age taking its toll on him, as well as the need to protect what he had created. So in 1987, on his eightieth birthday, he donated to the city of Spartanburg not only the gardens, but also the endowment to go with the gardens. And as an additional arrangement for the maintenance of the gardens, the Men's Garden Club of Spartanburg created the Spartanburg County Foundation.

Wildflowers bloom everywhere during the early spring. And of course azaleas, rhododendrons, and **mountain laurels** add their blossoms. In the shade of **oaks, pines, maples,** and **black gums, pond** and **water lilies** thrive in the many ponds scattered throughout the gardens. **Ferns, ivy,** and **hostas** provide groundcover. It is hard to believe that the gardens we enjoy today were once a bleak eyesore.

Rose Hill Plantation State Historic Site

Rose gardens and boxwood hedges under magnolias and oaks surround the former home of South Carolina "Secession Governor" William Henry Gist.

Address: 2677 Sardis Road, Union, SC 29379
Directions: From I-26 take exit 44 and go on SC 49 towards Union. After you cross SC 56 make a right turn onto Sardis Road and continue for about eight miles. The plantation entrance will be on your left.
Hours: grounds: 9:00 a.m. to 6:00 p.m. Thursday to Monday.; closed Tuesdays and Wednesdays; mansion: 1:00 p.m. to 4:00 p.m. Thursday, Friday, and Monday; 11:00 a.m. to 4:00 p.m. Saturday; noon to 4:00 p.m. Sunday or by appointment
Admission fee: grounds, no; mansion, yes
Wheelchair access: grounds, yes; mansion, no
Facilities: none
Area: 44 acres
Phone: (864) 427-5966

One of the smallest South Carolina state parks is located just a few miles outside of Union. But it is certainly not small on history. This forty-four-acre park features the former home of William Henry Gist, also known as South Carolina's "Secession Governor." The mansion was completed in 1832 on Gist's eight-thousand-acre cotton plantation. In the 1850s, rose gardens surrounded by boxwood hedges were planted. Gist was governor of South Carolina at the outbreak of the Civil War and he voted that South Carolina secede from the Union. Despite that, his mansion survived the war intact, which cannot be said about the homes of many other prominent South Carolina citizens. President Andrew Jackson pardoned Gist after the Civil War, but only after he had pledged loyalty to the United States. Gist died at Rose Hill Plantation but his wife continued to operate the plantation, which by this time barely covered two thousand acres. After her death in 1889, the

property was divided
among the Gists'
grandchildren
and gradually fell
into neglect and
disrepair. This sad
situation
continued until
the 1940s,
when the Rose Hill
Plantation was purchased by the Franks
family and gradually restored to its previous splendor and glory. The
state of South Carolina acquired the property in 1960 and designated
Rose Hill Plantation as a state park.

As you approach the mansion, you will enjoy beautiful
dogwoods along the driveway. A rose garden containing a large
number of **climbing roses** is located near the mansion and
boxwood hedges are everywhere. **Azaleas, gardenias**, and **camellias** add color and fragrance while **oaks** and **magnolias** provide
welcome shade. Huge **Southern magnolias** (*Magnolia grandiflora*)
towering in front of the mansion were planted at the time of its
construction. A beautiful hardwood grove is not far from the
mansion, and we found some of the **pecan trees** (*Carya illioniensis*) to
be magnificent specimens. You can explore further away from the
mansion on the easy, one-mile nature trail. This garden is listed on
the National Register of Historic Places.

Worth Seeing: Take a guided tour of the restored, 1832 Federal-style
mansion, featuring the original wooden-peg staircase and Renais-
sance Revival furnishings, as well as some family belongings.

Other Places of Interest to Garden and Plant Lovers

Coastal Region

Angel Oak
3688 Angel Oak Road
Johns Island, SC 29455
(843) 559-3496
The Angel Oak, an impressive live oak (*Quercus virginiana*), is really a tree to see. The property on which Angel Oak stands was originally part of a land grant given to Abraham Waight in 1717. A long and illustrious history followed. The city of Charleston acquired the property in 1991 and opened it to the public, free of charge, the same year. The age of Angel Oak is estimated to be at least 1,400 years, and its largest limbs rest on the ground. It is 65 feet high and has a circumference of 25.5 feet. The largest limb is 89 feet long and has a circumference of 11.25 feet. The oak provides an area of shade that is 17,000 square feet.

Battery and White Point Gardens
Charleston Department of Parks and Recreation
30 Mary Murray Drive
Charleston, SC 29403
(843) 724-7321
This park is located at the southern end of the city, along South Battery and King Streets. According to the city's earliest records, the names of White Point and Oyster Point were given to this area because of the white sand and oyster shells found in great quantities. The name "battery" commemorates the batteries placed on this site during the Revolutionary War, the War of 1812, and the Civil War. Designed according to the plans of architects Charles F. Reichardt and John Charles Olmstead, the park became an expanse of green lawn with statues, under a beautiful canopy of live oak trees.

Edisto Beach State Park
8377 State Cabin Road
Edisto Island, SC 29438
(843) 869-2156
A 1,255-acre park with 1.5 miles of beach. Visitors can observe life in the marsh, explore a dense live oak forest, or admire some of the tallest palmetto trees in South Carolina.

Francis Beidler Forest
336 Sanctuary Road
Harleyville, SC 29448
(843) 462-2150
It is hard to believe that Francis Beidler, one of America's first conservationists, was a lumberman. He certainly was a visionary, however. He is responsible for saving the only virgin, blackwater bald cypress and tupelo gum swamp forest left in the world. When he acquired his holdings in Four Holes Swamp in the 1890s, he allowed much of his timber to stand. For fifty years, up to his death in 1924, he championed the conservation of our country's natural beauty, and he did this long before it was popular or fashionable. After Beidler's death, his family continued to preserve his land holdings. Then in the 1960s, when the threat of logging emerged again in this area, the National Audubon Society and the Nature Conservancy joined forces and purchased this acreage. They purchased the surrounding wetlands as well, thus ensuring that the beauty of this area will be forever preserved for everyone to enjoy. Today this sanctuary encompasses 11,000 acres. A 1.5-mile boardwalk that begins at the visitor center traverses only a small part of the swamp but offers a very close view of trees, plants, and even occasional wildlife. You will see giant, ancient, cypress trees, some 1,000 years old and ten stories tall. The understory tupelo, blackgum, oak, and ash grow as high as seventy feet. The sanctuary also supports over three hundred species of wildlife. Do not miss the displays and exhibits in the visitor center, since they will prepare you for your wilderness walk.

Hampton Park

Charleston Department of Parks and Recreation
30 Mary Murray Drive
Charleston, SC 29403
(843) 724-7321

With ancient live oaks, magnolias, camellias, azaleas, a formal rose walk with over one hundred varieties of roses, and Sunken Gardens, this city park was named in honor of General Wade Hampton for his services to the state of South Carolina. Originally it was John Gibbes' Orange Grove Plantation in the 1700s, then the site of the Carolina Interstate and West Indian Exposition in 1902.

Hampton Plantation State Historic Site

1950 Rutledge Road
McClellanville, SC 29458
(843) 546-9361

This 322-acre property was once the centerpiece of a coastal rice plantation. The restored mansion, one of the finest examples of Georgian architecture, was formerly the home of Archibald Rutledge, South Carolina's first poet laureate. Over the past 250+ years, this mansion has hosted many famous patriots, politicians, and soldiers, including George Washington and Marquis de Lafayette. Enjoy the Dogwood and Holly 2.5-mile nature trail. This site is listed on the National Register of Historic Places and is also a National Historic Landmark.

Hopsewee Plantation

494 Hopsewee Road
Georgetown, SC 29440
(843) 546-7891

The house, built over 250 years ago, is a typical, low-country, rice plantation dwelling built of black cypress on a brick foundation covered by scored tabby. It is amazing to realize that this house was built almost forty years before the Revolutionary War and that only four families have owned it. It was home to Thomas Lynch Sr. and the birthplace of Thomas Lynch Jr., both distinguished political figures and the only father and son to serve in the Continental Congress. Thomas Jr. was a signer of the

Declaration of Independence, but Thomas Sr. suffered a stroke and was unable to sign. There is a space left on the document for his signature. A woodland trail along the North Santee River winds through a forest of moss-covered live oaks, pine, and hardwoods with many native plants. A National Historic Landmark.

Hunting Island State Park
2555 Sea Island Parkway
Hunting Island, SC 29920
(843) 838-2011
The island got its name because it was once used for hunting deer, waterfowl, and small game. It is a large barrier island with a wide, semi-tropical variety of plants. Observe the wildlife from the boardwalk extending far into the salt marsh. The lighthouse is listed on the National Register of Historic Places and is the only lighthouse in South Carolina that is open to public.

Huntington Beach State Park
16148 Ocean Highway
Murrells Inlet, SC 29576
(843) 237-4440
Visitors can observe the diverse natural environment of the South Carolina coast, ranging from beach to salt marsh to a freshwater lagoon. This 2,500-acre park has nature trails and boardwalks extending into the salt marsh and a freshwater lagoon for wildlife viewing. Visit the historic castle Atalaya, which served as the winter home and studio of the renowned American sculptress Anna Hyatt Huntington. Atalaya is a National Historic Landmark.

Lake Warren State Park
1079 Lake Warren Road
Hampton, SC 29924
(803) 943-5051
Large tracts of woodlands and wetlands support a large variety of plant species and wildlife habitats. The park encompasses 422 acres and features a two-hundred-acre lake, floodplain forest, and four species of pines.

Little Pee Dee State Park
1298 State Park Road
Dillon, SC 29536
(843) 774-8872
This 835-acre park also has a fifty-five-acre lake. Explore the river swamp along the scenic Little Pee Dee River. The 1.25-mile loop Beaver Pond nature trail winds through the Sandhills area, which offers a variety of trees and plants.

Lynches River State Park
1110 Ben Gause Road
Coward, SC 29530
(843) 389-2785
This 668-acre park is located on Lynches River in the Pee Dee region. Explore the meandering nature trails and see towering cypress trees growing in a river swamp. Sandhills also offers a wide variety of interesting vegetation.

Poinsett State Park
6660 Poinsett Park Road
Wedgefield, SC 29168
(803) 494-8177
The terrain of this 1,000-acre park allows for a remarkable diversity of plant and animal life. Different plant communities are represented here—pine-hardwood, swamps, sandhills, and mountain bluffs. Explore several nature trails and see bald cypress and tupelo trees tower above the swamp or the mountain laurel on the hillsides. The nature center features displays on native Sumter County plants, animals, and history. There is even a full-time naturalist here.

Santee National Wildlife Refuge
Santee NWR c/o Cape Romain NWR
5801 Highway 17
North Awendaw, SC 29429
(803) 478-2217
This National Wildlife Refuge was initially established to provide migratory waterfowl with a wintering habitat. Its current purpose is to provide habitat for endangered or threat-

ened species of red-cockaded woodpecker, Southern bald eagle, peregrine falcon, and American alligator. A one-mile nature trail winds through various habitats of this refuge. Do not forget to see Santee Indian Mound/Fort Watson, listed on the National Register of Historic Places.

Sergeant Jasper State Park
Route 2, Box 395
Hardeeville, SC 29927
(843) 784-5130
This park supports a wide variety of plant and waterfowl species on its 442 acres. There are several small lakes and a pine wetland habitat. The park is named for Revolutionary War hero Sgt. William Jasper. It is said that during the Battle of Fort Moultrie, while under heavy fire, he retrieved the fallen American flag and remounted it on the fort.

Woods Bay State Park
11020 Woods Bay Road
Olanta, SC 29114
(843) 659-4445
The main feature of this 1,541-acre state park is a geologic formation known as Carolina Bay. It offers a variety of swampy, natural habitats for many species of wildlife. Visit the Nature Center. Explore by nature trail or by boardwalk.

Piedmont Region

Aiken State Park
1145 State Park Road
Windsor, SC 29856
(803) 649-2857
Explore the nature trail and encounter a variety of animal and plant life at this park, 1,067 acres of which are a combination of dry sandhills and a river swamp.

Caesars Head State Park
8155 Geer Highway
Cleveland, SC 29635
(864) 836-6115
This park is a mecca for photographers and nature enthusiasts alike. Wildflowers blossom everywhere in all seasons, and Raven Cliff Falls is one of the highest waterfalls in the eastern United States.

Carolina Sandhills National Wildlife Refuge
Route 2, P.O. Box 330
McBee, SC 29101
(803) 335-8401
This refuge is situated in the transition zone between the Coastal Plain and the Piedmont Plateau. A multitude of plants thrives in this refuge. You will see longleaf and loblolly pines and turkey and bluejack oaks, as well as several species of sundews and pitcher plants. There are about 190 species of birds. The refuge supports about one hundred colonies of the endangered red-cockaded woodpecker, and it is not unusual to see bald eagles or gold eagles. Forty-two species of reptiles and twenty-five species of amphibians live in this refuge as well.

Congaree Swamp National Monument
200 Caroline Sims Road
Hopkins, SC 29061
(803) 776-4396
The 22,200-acre Congaree Swamp lies just about twenty miles

southeast of Columbia. It is a swamp forest stretching along the Congaree River and it is the last significant stand of old-growth river-bottom hardwood forest in the United States. This area found its protection when it was inducted into the National Park System in 1976. The area boasts about ninety tree species, many of which are state champion trees. A champion tree is the largest of its kind in the state, as determined by calculating its height, girth, and spread. A tree will remain a champion tree until a larger specimen is found. There are some beautiful specimens of bald cypress (*Taxodium distichum*) here. Some of them are over one hundred feet tall and the largest has a circumference of slightly more than twenty-seven feet. Some of the cypress knees are 7.5 feet high. A state champion loblolly pine (*Pinus taeda*) is 145 feet tall, more than 15 feet in circumference, and may be 250 to 300 years old. Loblolly pines as tall as 169 feet have been recorded. All eight woodpecker species found in the Southeast, including the endangered red-cockaded woodpecker, can be seen here. You can view the flora and fauna from twenty-five miles of trails. Colored markers make it easy to follow the park's six trails. There are two elevated boardwalks as well. Guided nature walks are available.

Goodale State Park
650 Park Road
Camden, SC 29020
(803) 432-2772
The 763-acre park features a spring-fed lake with beautiful cypress trees. Waterbirds and other wildlife abound. Explore the surrounding plant communities by nature trails.

Henry Timrod Park
City of Florence Park Division
180 North Irby Street
Florence, SC 29501
(843) 665-3270
This eighteen-acre park is named for Henry Timrod, the Poet Laureate of the Confederacy. Established in 1925, it is part of a twelve-park system totaling more than 180 acres. Enjoy the tree identification trail, formal gardens, and gazebo.

Jones Gap State Park

303 Jones Gap Road
Marietta, SC 29661
(864) 836-3647

Located in the 10,000-acre Mountain Bridge Wilderness Area, this 3,346-acre park represents one of the least-spoiled wilderness areas in South Carolina's upcountry. The Middle Saluda River flowing through the park was designated the state's first scenic river. More than four hundred species of plants, many of them rare or endangered, as well as state champion trees can be found here. There are fifty-two miles of hiking trails in this area.

Keowee-Toxaway State Park

108 Residence Drive
Sunset, SC 29685
(864) 868-2605

This 1,000-acre park features spectacular rock outcroppings and breathtaking views of the Foothills and Blue Ridge Mountains. Rhododendrons and mountain laurels thrive along the streams. The Interpretive Center features displays on the history and culture of the Cherokee Indians who once lived in this area. There are several hiking trails as well as the Cherokee Interpretive trail.

Lake Wateree State Park

881 State Park Road
Winnsboro, SC 29180
(803) 482-6401

Situated on Lake Wateree, this 238-acre park provides habitat for several bird species including blue herons, egrets, wood ducks, and mallards. There is an abundance of other wildlife as well. Explore the one-mile loop Deportes Island nature trail.

Landsford Canal State Park

2051 Park Drive
Catawba, SC 29704
(803) 789-5800

Landsford Canal is the best preserved of the South Carolina nineteenth-century canals. This 460-acre park contains remnants of

1820s canal locks, culverts, bridges, and locks. The lockkeeper's house explains the canal system of the Catawba and Wateree Rivers of South Carolina. These canals were used by boats to bypass the rapids when carrying cargo to and from the coast. The rocky shoals of the Catawba River are home to one of the world's largest populations of rocky shoal spider lilies. They are usually in full bloom in May. Listed on the National Register of Historic Places.

Lee State Park
487 Loop Road
Bishopville, SC 29010
(803) 428-3833
Lee State Park is a gateway to the scenic Lynches River. Its 2,839 acres support a wide variety of plant and animal species. It features an extensive hardwood floodplain forest, sandhills habitat, and several artesian springs. There is also a nature trail.

Lucas Park
City of Florence Park Division
180 North Irby Street
Florence, SC 29501
(843) 665-3270
A twelve-acre park named for Florence businessman Marion D. Lucas. In the early 1960s, more than 10,000 azaleas and camellias were planted here. And when you visit in the spring you will certainly enjoy the blossoms of redbuds, dogwoods, and wisteria.

Redcliffe State Historic Site
181 Redcliffe Road
Beech Island, SC 29842
(803) 827-1473
Redcliffe was the homeplace of James H. Hammond and three generations of his descendents. Hammond was a successful cotton planter and governor of South Carolina. Many original works of art and furnishings can be seen in the mansion today. The surrounding 369 acres of grounds are heavily wooded and there are many historic plantings. The lane of magnolias lining the entrance to the estate is truly memorable. Do not forget to

explore the nature trail as well. Redcliffe is listed on the National Register of Historic Places.

Sesquicentennial State Park
9564 Two Notch Road
Columbia, SC 29223
(803) 788-2706
This state park is situated in the middle of the sandhills region. It encompasses 1,419 acres, including a thirty-acre lake, and is surrounded by nature trails. There is a nature center and the park naturalist provides nature programs year-round.

Walnut Grove Plantation
1200 Otts Shoal Drive
Roebuck, SC 29376
(864) 576-6546
King George III deeded Walnut Grove Plantation to Charles Moore at a time when this area was just a wild frontier. Moore's children were Revolutionary War heroes. Today you can see all the original plantation buildings. Do not miss the Moravian-built Conestoga wagon that was made to float the rivers or act as a cart. Take the guided tour or go on your own. The self-guided tour, with its detailed listing of points of interest, will lead you through a nature trail, an old cemetery, and even an herb garden. A registered National Historic Landmark.

Woodrow Wilson Boyhood Home
1705 Hampton Street
Columbia, SC 29201
(803) 252-1770
This was the home of Thomas Woodrow Wilson, twenty-eighth president of the United States, who lived in Columbia as a teenager from 1870 until 1874. Although this was a relatively short period of time, these years were the turning point of his life. His father was a Presbyterian minister who taught at the Columbia Theological Seminary. He preached at the carriage house on the grounds of the Seminary, which served as a chapel for the seminary students. Woodrow Wilson later remembered these services as the most important in his life. The house, built

in the mode of a Tuscan villa, is surrounded by a white picket fence. It is furnished in the Victorian style and contains some Wilson family memorabilia. The gardens surrounding the house have been restored by the Columbia Garden Club to resemble as much as possible the Wilsons' gardens. Mrs. Wilson planted the magnolia trees, dogwoods, and tea olive. There are plantings of roses and a small gazebo.

Where to See Specific Types of Flora

Note: This listing only includes gardens with major displays.

Azaleas:
Middleton Place
Magnolia Plantation and Gardens
Summerville Azalea Garden
Nancy Bryan Luce Gardens
Glencairn Garden
Cypress Gardens

Camellias:
Magnolia Plantation and Gardens
Middleton Place
South Carolina Botanical Garden
Hopeland Gardens

Daylilies:
Riverbanks Botanical Garden
Kalmia Gardens of Coker College

Flowering trees:
Brookgreen Gardens
Magnolia Plantation and Gardens
Middleton Place

Herb gardens:
Magnolia Plantation and Gardens
Kalmia Gardens of Coker College
Park Seed Company Garden

Irises:
Swan Lake Iris Gardens

Japanese gardens:
Japanese Garden of Furman University
Wells Japanese Garden

Maze garden:
Magnolia Plantation and Gardens

Mountain laurels:	Kalmia Gardens of Coker College
Rhododendrons:	Kalmia Gardens of Coker College South Carolina Botanical Garden
Rose gardens:	Edisto Memorial Gardens Middleton Place Riverbanks Botanical Garden Park Seed Company Trial Gardens Hopeland Gardens
Vegetable gardens:	Park Seed Company Trial Gardens
Water lilies:	Cypress Gardens

A Calendar of South Carolina Garden Events

April

South Carolina Festival of Roses
Edisto Memorial Gardens
(803) 534-6821

"Come See Me" Festival
Glencairn Garden
(803) 329-5620

Daffodil Festival
South Carolina Botanical Garden
(864) 656-3405

May

Annual Flowertown Festival
Summerville Azalea Garden
(843) 871-9622

Iris Festival
Swan Lake Iris Gardens
(803) 773-3371

June

South Carolina Festival of Flowers
Greenwood Chamber of Commerce
(864) 223-8411

Index